103 Uses For Your
Turkey Fryer

RECIPES & IDEAS FOR THE OTHER 364 DAYS OF THE YEAR

Printed in the United States of America
by G&R Publishing Co.

Distributed By:

CQProducts

507 Industrial Street
Waverly, IA 50677

ISBN-13: 978-1-56383-203-1
ISBN-10: 1-56383-203-8
Item #7007

Table of Contents

Tips & Suggestions
For Frying A Turkey:

Note 1:
When cooking with oil, use only oil with high smoke points, such as peanut, canola or saffl ower oil.

Note 2:
To determine the correct amount of oil, place the turkey in the fryer (before adding any seasonings) and fi ll the pot with water until the turkey is covered. Remove turkey and measure the amount of water in the fryer. Use the corresponding amount of oil when frying the turkey. Dry the fryer thoroughly of all water before adding oil or storing.

Note 3:
Never fry a turkey indoors, in a garage or under a structure attached to a building. Do not fry turkey on wooden decks, which could catch fi re. Frying a turkey over concrete could cause stains on the concrete from the oil. It is best to fry a turkey on a level dirt or grassy area. Always keep a fi re extinguisher nearby when frying a turkey. It is wise to have two people lowering and raising the turkey. To prevent burns caused by the splattering oil, always wear oven mitts or gloves, long sleeves and even glasses.

Note 4:
Let hot oil cool completely before transferring to storage containers or disposing. Cooled oil can be transferred to empty, clean milk jugs or buckets and stored in a refrigerator. Once oil has been used for cooking, it should be treated as a meat product and kept cool in a refrigerator. If properly stored, oil can be safely used up to 3 times. Signs of oil deterioration include foaming, darkening or excessive smoking.

Safety First:

Remember, safety fi rst! Some important equipment to use and have on hand are heavy duty long gloves, a face shield or safety glasses, a fi re extinguisher and bucket of sand.

Be sure to read and follow all of the manufacturer's instructions when using your turkey fryer and propane tank.

Never leave the turkey fryer unattended and keep careful watch during the cooking process. Should a grease fi re occur, immediately turn off the gas and cover the pot with a lid. If the oil begins to smoke, immediately turn off the gas.

Use your turkey fryer outdoors in an open area away from houses, garages, sheds, decks, trees, shrubs, children and pets.

Always make sure there is at least 2 feet of space between the propane tank and the fryer burner. Place the tank and fryer so that any wind will blow the heat of the fryer away from the gas tank.

Always center the fryer pot, Dutch oven or wok over the burner of the turkey fryer.

Immediately wash hands, utensils, equipment, gloves and any surfaces that have come in contact with a raw turkey or other raw meat.

Ideas & Recipes for Spring

Vegetable Egg Rolls

Makes 48 rolls

6 T. dark sesame oil
3 C. shredded carrots
3 C. thinly sliced
  shitake mushrooms
3 C. snow peas, thinly
  sliced
3 tsp. fresh minced garlic
3 tsp. fresh minced
  gingerroot

3 C. finely shredded
  green cabbage
6 green onions, thinly
  sliced
¾ C. teriyaki sauce
Frying oil
3 (16 oz.) pkgs. egg
  roll wrappers
3 large eggs, well beaten

In a large skillet over medium high heat, heat sesame oil. Add shredded carrots, sliced mushrooms, snow peas, minced garlic and minced gingerroot. Sauté for 4 minutes and remove from heat. Let cool and add shredded cabbage, sliced green onions and teriyaki sauce. Mix well.

Pour frying oil into fryer pot. Set fryer to medium-high setting and heat oil to 350°F. It should take about 20+ minutes to heat the oil, depending on the amount of oil, outside temperature and wind conditions. Meanwhile, spoon ⅓ cup of the filling mixture into the center of each egg roll wrapper. Fold top corner down over filling and tuck under filling. Fold left and right corners over filling. Lightly brush remaining corner with beaten egg. Tightly roll filled end toward corner and press gently to seal.

When oil temperature reaches 350° on a deep-fry thermometer, slowly place egg rolls into the oil. Fry 10 to 12 egg rolls at a time.

Immediately check the oil temperature and increase the flame so the oil temperature is maintained at 350°. If the oil temperature drops to 340° or below, oil will begin to seep into the egg rolls. Fry egg rolls for 2 to 3 minutes or until golden brown, turning once. Remove egg rolls from oil and set on paper towels to drain. Serve warm.

Let hot oil cool completely before transferring to storage containers or disposing (see Note 4 on page 1).

Jalapeno Poppers

Makes 24 servings

Frying oil
48 fresh whole jalapeno
    peppers
48 slices Monterey Jack
    or Cheddar cheese,
    cut into 1½" strips

1 C. flour
2 T. Cajun seasoning
1½ C. buttermilk
Ranch dressing, optional

Pour frying oil into fryer pot. Set fryer to medium-high setting and heat oil to 350°F. It should take about 20+ minutes to heat the oil, depending on the amount of oil, outside temperature and wind conditions. Meanwhile, cut a slice in each pepper lengthwise on one side. Remove seeds and stuff each pepper with a piece of cheese.

In a medium bowl, using a whisk, combine flour and Cajun seasoning. Slowly pour buttermilk into flour mixture, stirring until smooth. Dip stuffed peppers into batter, coating on all sides.

When oil temperature reaches 350° on a deep-fry thermometer, slowly place 10 to 12 peppers into the oil.

Fry each batch of peppers for 2 minutes or until golden. Remove peppers from oil with a slotted spoon or using the fryer basket and set on paper towels to drain. If desired, serve with Ranch dressing.

Let hot oil cool completely before transferring to storage containers or disposing (see Note 4 on page 1).

Fried Okra

Makes 24 servings

Frying oil
4 lbs. okra
2 tsp. salt

6 C. buttermilk
8 C. cornmeal

Pour frying oil into fryer pot. Set fryer to medium-high setting and heat oil to 375°F. It should take about 25+ minutes to heat the oil, depending on the amount of oil, outside temperature and wind conditions. Meanwhile, thoroughly wash okra and place on paper towels to drain.

Remove tip and stem end of okra and cut okra into $\frac{1}{2}$" slices. Place okra slices in a large bowl and sprinkle with salt. Add buttermilk, stirring until fully covered. Let stand for 15 minutes and drain well. Place cornmeal in a large shallow dish and dredge okra slices into cornmeal until well coated.

When oil temperature reaches 375° on a deep-fry thermometer, slowly place some of the okra slices into the oil.

Fry each batch of okra until golden brown. Remove okra from oil with a slotted spoon or using the fryer basket and set on paper towels to drain.

Let hot oil cool completely before transferring to storage containers or disposing (see Note 4 on page 1).

Vegetables Tempura with Dipping Sauce

Makes 10 servings

Frying oil
2 sweet potatoes
2 red or green bell
  peppers
24 small mushrooms
2 large cucumbers

3 C. flour
3 tsp. baking powder
1 tsp. salt
2 egg whites
$2\frac{1}{2}$ C. ice water

Pour frying oil into fryer pot. Set fryer to medium-high setting and heat oil to 375°F. Meanwhile, cut vegetables into $\frac{1}{4}$" slices. In a large bowl, combine flour, baking powder and salt. In a separate bowl, combine egg whites and water. Sift the flour mixture into the egg whites, stirring until slightly lumpy.

Dip vegetables into the batter mixture, shaking off the excess. When oil temperature reaches 375° on a deep-fry thermometer, slowly place some of the vegetables into the oil.

Fry each batch of vegetables until golden brown. Remove vegetables from oil with a slotted spoon or using the fryer basket and set on paper towels to drain.

Let hot oil cool completely before transferring to storage containers or disposing (see Note 4 on page 1).

Dipping Sauce

Makes about 3 cups

2 C. chicken broth
$\frac{2}{3}$ C. soy sauce
$\frac{2}{3}$ C. dry sherry
3 tsp. sugar

2 tsp. fresh grated
  gingerroot
4 T. sliced green onions

In a medium saucepan over low heat, combine chicken broth, soy sauce, sherry, sugar and gingerroot. Bring to a boil, reduce heat and let simmer for 5 minutes. Remove from heat and let cool. Stir in sliced green onions.

Buffalo Wings

Makes 24 to 36 wings

Frying oil
1 T. butter
2 (12 oz.) bottles
    Louisiana Red Hot
    sauce
1 (5 oz.) bottle Tabasco
    sauce
Pinch of garlic powder

Pinch of Worcestershire
    sauce
Dash of soy sauce
1 T. ketchup
1 T. water
1 T. cornstarch
24 to 36 chicken wings

Pour frying oil into fryer pot. Set fryer to medium-high setting and heat oil to 350°F. It should take about 20+ minutes to heat the oil, depending on the amount of oil, outside temperature and wind conditions. Meanwhile, in a large saucepan over medium heat, place butter. When butter has melted, stir in Red Hot sauce, Tabasco sauce, garlic powder, Worcestershire sauce, soy sauce and ketchup. Let mixture simmer for 15 minutes. In a small bowl, combine water and cornstarch. Blend cornstarch mixture into hot sauce mixture until thickened.

When oil temperature reaches 350° on a deep-fry thermometer, slowly place the chicken wings into the oil.

Fry chicken wings until golden brown. Remove wings from oil and set on paper towels to drain. Place hot sauce mixture in a large plastic container with a tight fitting lid. Add drained chicken wings to hot sauce in the container. Close container with lid and shake until well coated.

Let hot oil cool completely before transferring to storage containers or disposing (see Note 4 on page 1).

Crispy Shrimp

Makes about 30 servings

Frying oil	4 T. Cajun seasoning
8 lbs. fresh or frozen	6 C. Bisquick baking mix
large shrimp	8 C. club soda
4 C. flour	

Pour frying oil into fryer pot. Set fryer to medium-high setting and heat oil to 350°F. It should take about 20+ minutes to heat the oil, depending on the amount of oil, outside temperature and wind conditions. Meanwhile, thaw shrimp completely and peel, leaving the tails intact. Devein shrimp, rinse and pat dry. In a medium bowl, combine flour and Cajun seasoning. In a separate bowl, combine baking mix and club soda. Coat shrimp in flour mixture, shaking off excess, and dip into batter mixture. Dredge shrimp again in flour.

When oil temperature reaches 350° on a deep-fry thermometer, slowly place coated shrimp in oil.

Fry shrimp for 2 to 3 minutes. Remove shrimp from oil with a slotted spoon or using the fryer basket and set on paper towels to drain.

Let hot oil cool completely before transferring to storage containers or disposing (see Note 4 on page 1).

Cajun Chicken Nuggets

Frying oil
2 lbs. boneless, skinless
   chicken breast halves
1 tsp. salt
1 tsp. pepper
2 eggs

$\frac{2}{3}$ C. club soda
$\frac{2}{3}$ C. flour
3 tsp. cayenne pepper
3 tsp. onion powder
2 tsp. dried thyme
2 tsp. garlic powder

Pour frying oil into fryer pot. Set fryer to medium-high setting and heat oil to 360°F. It should take about 25+ minutes to heat the oil, depending on the amount of oil, outside temperature and wind conditions. Meanwhile, cut chicken breast halves into $1\frac{1}{2}$" squares. Season chicken squares with salt and pepper. In a medium bowl, combine eggs and club soda. Add chicken pieces, turning until coated and let stand for 15 minutes, turning once. On a large sheet of waxed paper, combine flour, cayenne pepper, onion powder, dried thyme and garlic powder. Remove chicken pieces from egg mixture, shaking off excess and roll into seasoning on waxed paper. When all chicken pieces are coated, dip chicken pieces again into the egg mixture.

When oil temperature reaches 360° on a deep-fry thermometer, slowly place coated chicken nuggets in oil.

Fry nuggets for 5 to 6 minutes. Remove nuggets from oil with a slotted spoon or using the fryer basket and set on paper towels to drain.

Let hot oil cool completely before transferring to storage containers or disposing (see Note 4 on page 1).

Fried Clams

Makes 10 servings

Frying oil
8 C. shucked hard
  shelled clams
2 eggs

4 tsp. seafood seasoning
1 C. flour
2 C. dry bread crumbs

Pour frying oil into fryer pot. Set fryer to medium-high setting and heat oil to 375°F. It should take about 30+ minutes to heat the oil, depending on the amount of oil, outside temperature and wind conditions. Meanwhile, drain clams and reserve ¼ cup of the clam juice. In a medium bowl, combine eggs, seafood seasoning and reserved ¼ cup clam juice with a fork until well mixed. Place flour and dry bread crumbs into two separate shallow bowls. Dredge the clams in the flour and dip into the egg mixture. Roll the clams in the bread crumbs and place on a wire rack.

When oil temperature reaches 375° on a deep-fry thermometer, slowly place coated clams in oil.

Fry clams for 4 to 5 minutes. Remove clams from oil with a slotted spoon or using the fryer basket and set on paper towels to drain.

Let hot oil cool completely before transferring to storage containers or disposing (see Note 4 on page 1).

Cornish Hens

Makes 4 servings

1 T. kosher salt
¼ tsp. pepper
1 T. onion powder
1½ tsp. garlic powder
1 tsp. cayenne pepper

4 Cornish hens,
    completely thawed
2 gallons peanut oil
    (see Note 2 on page 1)

In a small bowl, combine kosher salt, pepper, onion powder, garlic powder and cayenne pepper. Stir until seasonings are fully combined.

Rub seasoning mixture to coat all surfaces of the Cornish hens. Place hens in the fryer basket or on the rack, neck side down.

Add measured amount of peanut oil to the fryer pot (see Note 2 on page 1). Set fryer to medium-high setting and heat oil to 350°F. It should take about 30+ minutes to heat the oil, depending on the amount of oil, outside temperature and wind conditions.

When oil temperature reaches 375° on a deep-fry thermometer, slowly lower hens into the oil.

Fry hens for about 3 minutes per pound plus 5 minutes, using the weight of the heaviest Cornish hen. For example, if the heaviest hen weighs 2 pounds. The cooking time would be 2 x 3 + 5, for a total cooking time of 11 minutes. Carefully remove the hens from the hot oil and let drain for about 10 minutes.

Let hot oil cool completely before transferring to storage containers or disposing (see Note 4 on page 1).

Fried Ravioli

Makes 24 servings

Frying oil
2 C. flavored croutons
4 large eggs
1 C. milk

4 (9 oz.) pkgs. refrigerated
  four cheese ravioli
Marinara sauce

Pour frying oil into fryer pot. Set fryer to medium-high setting and heat oil to 375°F. It should take about 30+ minutes to heat the oil, depending on the amount of oil, outside temperature and wind conditions. Meanwhile, in a blender, place croutons. Process croutons on high until finely ground. Place ground croutons in a shallow dish. In a medium bowl, combine eggs and milk. Dip ravioli in egg mixture and roll in crushed croutons.

When oil temperature reaches 375° on a deep-fry thermometer, slowly place coated ravioli in oil.

Fry ravioli for 8 to 10 minutes. Remove ravioli from oil with a slotted spoon or using the fryer basket and set on paper towels to drain. Serve ravioli with marinara sauce.

Let hot oil cool completely before transferring to storage containers or disposing (see Note 4 on page 1).

Fried Spinach Balls

Makes 18 servings

Frying oil
6 C. chopped, cooked
  spinach
6 T. butter, melted
6 T. minced onions
6 T. grated Parmesan
  cheese

Salt and pepper to taste
6 eggs, divided
5 C. dry bread crumbs,
  divided
$\frac{3}{8}$ tsp. allspice
$\frac{3}{4}$ C. water

Pour frying oil into fryer pot. Set fryer to medium-high setting and heat oil to 360°F. It should take about 20+ minutes to heat the oil, depending on the amount of oil, outside temperature and wind conditions. Meanwhile, in a large bowl, combine cooked spinach, melted butter, minced onions, Parmesan cheese, salt, pepper, 3 eggs, 3 cups bread crumbs and allspice. Mix well and let stand for 10 minutes. In a separate bowl, whisk together remaining 3 eggs and water. Place remaining 2 cups dry bread crumbs in a shallow dish. Roll spinach mixture into balls. Dip balls in egg mixture and then roll in bread crumbs.

When oil temperature reaches 360° on a deep-fry thermometer, slowly place spinach balls in oil.

Fry spinach balls until golden brown. Remove spinach balls from oil with a slotted spoon or using the fryer basket and set on paper towels to drain.

Let hot oil cool completely before transferring to storage containers or disposing (see Note 4 on page 1).

Lemon Donuts

Makes about 2 dozen donuts

4½ C. sifted flour	1 C. sugar
2 tsp. baking powder	3 T. butter, softened
1 tsp. baking soda	1 T. grated lemon peel
½ tsp. salt	1 C. buttermilk
¼ tsp. nutmeg	Frying oil
2 eggs	

In a medium bowl, combine flour, baking powder, baking soda, salt and nutmeg. Mix well. In a large mixing bowl, beat together the eggs, sugar, butter and lemon peel at medium speed until well blended. Alternating, add flour mixture and buttermilk to egg mixture. Cover bowl and refrigerate dough overnight. On a lightly floured flat surface, roll dough to $\frac{3}{8}$" thickness. Using a $2\frac{3}{4}$" donut cutter, cut donuts into circles. Place donuts and donut holes on a baking sheet. Re-roll the remaining dough and continue cutting out donuts. Place baking sheets with donuts in refrigerator while oil is heating.

Pour frying oil into fryer pot. Set fryer to medium-high setting and heat oil to 375°F. It should take about 30+ minutes to heat the oil, depending on the amount of oil, outside temperature and wind conditions.

When oil temperature reaches 375° on a deep-fry thermometer, slowly place donuts and donut holes in oil. Fry donuts for 2 to 3 minutes, turning once. Remove donuts from oil with a slotted spoon or using the fryer basket and set on paper towels to drain. Donut holes may need to be removed after 1 to 2 minutes of frying time.

Let hot oil cool completely before transferring to storage containers or disposing (see Note 4 on page 1).

PB Banana Sandwiches

Makes 16 servings

Frying oil

2 C. creamy or crunchy peanut butter

32 slices white bread

4 ripe bananas

9 C. Bisquick baking mix

5 C. water

Powdered sugar

Pour frying oil into fryer pot. Set fryer to medium-high setting and heat oil to 350°F. It should take about 20+ minutes to heat the oil, depending on the amount of oil, outside temperature and wind conditions. Meanwhile, spread about 2 tablespoons peanut butter over one side of half of the slices of bread. Cut each banana into 4 parts and slice each part into 3 parts. Place 3 banana slices on each of the peanut buttered slices. Top with remaining slices of bread to make 16 sandwiches. In a medium bowl, combine baking mix and water. Dip sandwiches into batter until well coated, shaking off excess.

When oil temperature reaches 375° on a deep-fry thermometer, slowly place coated sandwiches in oil.

Place sandwiches in fryer and push down on sandwiches with long tongs for 30 seconds. Let sandwiches float to the top and fry for 2 minutes, turning once. Remove sandwiches from oil with long tongs and set on paper towels to drain. Lightly sprinkle sandwiches with powdered sugar.

Let hot oil cool completely before transferring to storage containers or disposing (see Note 4 on page 1).

Naturally-Dyed Easter Eggs

Makes 4 dozen eggs

4 dozen eggs   2 tsp. vinegar
Water to cover

　　To dye Easter eggs using natural products, use the following products to reach the desired color.

Fresh beets or cranberries: pale red
Yellow onion skins: orange
Orange or lemon peels: light yellow
Ground turmeric: yellow
Spinach leaves: pale green
Yellow Delicious apple peels: greenish gold
Canned blueberries or red cabbage leaves: blue

　　Place eggs in the bottom of the turkey fryer pot and add water to cover eggs. Set burner to low and bring water to a boil. Reduce heat and let simmer for 15 minutes. After 5 minutes, add vinegar and ingredient(s) from the list above to reach desired dye color. Reduce fryer setting to very low. Once eggs have reached desired shade, carefully remove eggs from turkey fryer and let drain on wire racks. Discard water and dye ingredients and thoroughly rinse fryer pot.

Tie Dye

Water
Lemon yellow, fuchsia
   and turquoise dye*

Various white clothing
   garments
Rubber bands

   Fill the turkey fryer pot with water and add dye according to package directions. Mix dyes according to the chart below to make desired colors. Wrap rubber bands tightly around white clothing, such as t-shirts, tank tops and shorts. Wherever the rubber bands are placed, there will be a white marking on the clothing. Submerge the clothing pieces in the dyed water, pushing down with long tongs or a stick. Let clothing sit in dye for at least 15 to 20 minutes. The longer the clothing remains in the dye, the darker the color will become. Remove clothing from dye and rinse under cool water, according to dye package directions. Ring out garments until water runs clear. Carefully remove rubber bands by using a scissors to cut them from the dye garments. Let dyed garments dry completely.

*You should be able to make a wide array of colors from mixing yellow, fuchsia and turquoise dye. For example,
4 parts fuchsia and 1 part yellow: red
1 part red and 1 part yellow: orange
1 part yellow and 2 parts turquoise: green
4 parts turquoise and 1 part fuchsia: blue
2 parts turquoise and 1 part fuchsia: purple

Ideas &
Recipes for
Summer

Popcorn Shrimp

Makes 16 servings

Frying oil
4 lbs. small shrimp,
   peeled and deveined
4 eggs
4 tsp. salt
4 tsp. cayenne pepper

2 tsp. garlic powder
1 tsp. dried thyme
1 tsp. dried oregano
½ tsp. pepper
2 C. flour
4 C. cornmeal

Pour frying oil into fryer pot. Set fryer to medium-high setting and heat oil to 375°F. It should take about 30+ minutes to heat the oil, depending on the amount of oil, outside temperature and wind conditions. Meanwhile, rinse shrimp under cool water and pat dry completely. In a medium bowl, combine eggs, salt, cayenne pepper, garlic powder, dried thyme, dried oregano and pepper, beating until frothy. On two separate large sheets of waxed paper, place flour and cornmeal. Dredge the shrimp in the flour and dip in the egg mixture. Roll shrimp in cornmeal and place on wire racks until all shrimp are coated.

When oil temperature reaches 375° on a deep-fry thermometer, slowly place coated shrimp into the oil.

Fry each batch of shrimp for 1 to 2 minutes or until golden. Remove shrimp from oil with a slotted spoon or using the fryer basket and set on paper towels to drain.

Let hot oil cool completely before transferring to storage containers or disposing (see Note 4 on page 1).

Apple BBQ Sauce

Makes 2 gallons

8 C. ketchup
2 T. white pepper
4 C. apple juice
   concentrate
2¾ C. peeled diced
   apples

2 C. apple cider vinegar
2 C. diced onions
2 C. soy sauce
5½ tsp. diced green
   peppers
2 T. garlic powder

In the turkey fryer pot, combine ketchup, white pepper, apple juice concentrate, diced apples, apple cider vinegar, diced onions, soy sauce, diced green peppers and garlic powder. Set fryer setting to low and bring sauce to a boil, stirring frequently with a long spoon. Reduce heat to very low and let simmer for 15 minutes, stirring frequently. If smooth sauce is preferred, carefully transfer sauce to a blender or food processor in batches and puree until smooth. Using a funnel, transfer sauce to gallon jugs. Cover jugs tightly and store sauce in refrigerator until ready to use.

Fried Dill Pickles

Makes 2 dozen servings

Frying oil
2 (32 oz.) jars sliced
    dill pickles

4 C. cornmeal
1 T. Cajun seasoning

Pour frying oil into fryer pot. Set fryer to medium-high setting and heat oil to 350°F. It should take about 20+ minutes to heat the oil, depending on the amount of oil, outside temperature and wind conditions. Meanwhile, drain pickles, rinse and pat dry completely. In a large plastic bag, combine cornmeal and Cajun seasoning. Add drained pickles to bag. May have to coat pickles in batches. Seal bag and shake until well coated.

When oil temperature reaches 350° on a deep-fry thermometer, slowly place coated pickles into the oil.

Fry each batch of pickles for 1 to 2 minutes or until golden. Remove pickles from oil with a slotted spoon or using the fryer basket and set on paper towels to drain.

Let hot oil cool completely before transferring to storage containers or disposing (see Note 4 on page 1).

Deep Fried Cauliflower, Mushrooms & Zucchini

Makes 30 servings

Frying oil	2 large zucchini
2 large heads cauliflower	6 C. dry bread crumbs
2 (16 oz.) pkgs.	6 large eggs
whole mushrooms	1 C. milk

Pour frying oil into fryer pot. Set fryer to medium-high setting and heat oil to 375°F. It should take about 30+ minutes to heat the oil, depending on the amount of oil, outside temperature and wind conditions. Meanwhile, remove outer leaves from cauliflower. Rinse cauliflower, mushrooms and zucchinis under cool water and pat dry completely. Break cauliflower into small florets and cut zucchinis into $\frac{1}{2}$" thick slices. In a shallow bowl, place bread crumbs. In a separate bowl, using a whisk, thoroughly combine eggs and milk. Dip cauliflower florets, mushrooms and zucchini slices into egg mixture. Roll vegetables in bread crumbs until fully coated.

When oil temperature reaches 375° on a deep-fry thermometer, slowly place coated vegetables into the oil.

Fry each batch of vegetables for 1 to 2 minutes or until golden. Remove vegetables from oil with a slotted spoon or using the fryer basket and set on paper towels to drain.

Let hot oil cool completely before transferring to storage containers or disposing (see Note 4 on page 1).

Funnel Cakes

Makes about 15 cakes

Frying oil	8 C. flour
8 eggs, lightly beaten	2 T. baking powder
6 C. milk	1 tsp. salt
1 C. brown sugar	Powdered sugar for dusting

Pour frying oil into fryer pot. Set fryer to medium-high setting and heat oil to 375°F. It should take about 30+ minutes to heat the oil, depending on the amount of oil, outside temperature and wind conditions. Meanwhile, in a medium bowl, combine eggs, milk and brown sugar. In a separate bowl, combine flour, baking powder and salt. Add egg mixture to flour mixture, stirring until well combined.

When oil temperature reaches 375° on a deep-fry thermometer, place 1 cup of the batter into a funnel, holding finger over the funnel spout so the batter does not drip through the funnel. Carefully hold funnel several inches above the hot oil and release finger so batter falls into hot oil. Quickly move funnel in a spiral motion until all of the batter is released.

Fry funnel cake for 2 minutes on each side, flipping carefully with long tongs. Remove funnel cake from oil with long tongs and set on paper towels to drain. Repeat with remaining batter. Sift powdered sugar over funnel cakes.

Let hot oil cool completely before transferring to storage containers or disposing (see Note 4 on page 1).

Pineapple Rings

Makes 12 servings

Frying oil
2 (20 oz.) cans pineapple
  rings

2 large eggs
½ C. flour

Pour frying oil into fryer pot. Set fryer to medium-high setting and heat oil to 350°F. It should take about 20+ minutes to heat the oil, depending on the amount of oil, outside temperature and wind conditions. Meanwhile, drain pineapple rings completely. In a medium bowl, combine eggs and flour, mixing until a thick paste forms. Dip pineapple rings in batter mixture, shaking off excess.

When oil temperature reaches 350° on a deep-fry thermometer, slowly place coated pineapple rings into the oil.

Fry pineapple rings for 1 to 2 minutes on each side, flipping carefully with long tongs. Remove pineapple rings from oil with long tongs and set on paper towels to drain.

Let hot oil cool completely before transferring to storage containers or disposing (see Note 4 on page 1).

Cree Indian Bannock Cakes

Makes about 20 cakes

Frying oil
8 C. flour
2 tsp. salt
6 T. baking powder

1 C. raisins, optional
¼ C. vegetable oil
3 C. water

Pour frying oil into fryer pot. Set fryer to medium-high setting and heat oil to 350°F. It should take about 20+ minutes to heat the oil, depending on the amount of oil, outside temperature and wind conditions. Meanwhile, in a large bowl, combine flour, salt, baking powder and, if desired, raisins. Make a well in the center of the dry ingredients and add vegetable oil and water. Mix well until a dough forms, adding a little water if needed. Dough should be the consistency of bread dough. On a lightly floured flat surface, knead dough until lumps are gone, being careful not to handle the dough too much. Roll tablespoonfuls of dough into small balls and flatten each ball into a 3" circle. Cut two slits in the center of each circle, which will make the bannock cook evenly.

When oil temperature reaches 350° on a deep-fry thermometer, slowly place small cakes into the oil.

Fry cakes for 3 to 5 minutes or until golden brown. Remove cakes from oil with a slotted spoon or using the fryer basket and set on paper towels to drain.

Let hot oil cool completely before transferring to storage containers or disposing (see Note 4 on page 1).

Fried Ice Cream

Makes 16 servings

2 C. finely chopped
   pecans
2 quarts vanilla ice
   cream, slightly
   softened

6 large eggs
4 C. finely crushed
   vanilla wafers
Frying oil

Line two baking sheets with waxed paper. Place chopped pecans in a shallow dish. Scoop vanilla ice cream into sixteen $\frac{1}{2}$ cup balls, rounding with an ice cream scoop. Roll ice cream balls in pecans until fully coated. Place ice cream balls on prepared baking sheets and place in freezer overnight.

Meanwhile, place beaten eggs in a bowl and place crushed vanilla wafers in a shallow dish. Dip each ice cream ball in the egg mixture and roll in crushed wafers until fully covered and return to freezer for 3 hours.

Pour frying oil into fryer pot. Set fryer to medium-high setting and heat oil to 375°F. It should take about 30+ minutes to heat the oil, depending on the amount of oil, outside temperature and wind conditions.

When oil temperature reaches 375° on a deep-fry thermometer, slowly place ice cream ball into the oil.

Fry ice cream for 30 to 45 seconds or until outside is crispy. Remove ice cream from oil with a slotted spoon and place on serving dishes. Serve immediately.

Let hot oil cool completely before transferring to storage containers or disposing (see Note 4 on page 1).

Steamed Halibut

Makes 3 pounds

6 green onions, chopped
12 fresh mushrooms, sliced
12 Napa cabbage leaves, sliced
2 T. fresh minced gingerroot
4 cloves garlic, minced
3 lbs. halibut fillets, or other fish
$\frac{1}{2}$ C. soy sauce
$\frac{1}{4}$ C. water
Crushed red pepper flakes to taste

Fill turkey fryer pot with 2" water and place fryer setting to medium heat. Bring water to a boil. Meanwhile, line the bottom of the turkey fryer basket with aluminum foil, folding up the aluminum foil to cover the sides of the basket as well. Arrange green onions, mushroom slices, cabbage slices, minced gingerroot and minced garlic into fryer basket over aluminum foil. Place halibut fillets over vegetables in basket. Drizzle soy sauce and water over fish and vegetables. When water is boiling in fryer pot, place filled basket in fryer and cover fryer with lid. Steam fish and vegetables for 15 to 20 minutes, or until fish flakes easily with a fork.

Rack of Ribs

Makes 4 to 6 racks

4 to 6 (2 lb.) racks   ¼ C. minced garlic
    of ribs   2 T. dried thyme
Water   ¼ C. celery salt
½ C. salt

Place racks of ribs in turkey fryer pot and fill with water to cover. Remove ribs from water and stir salt, minced garlic, dried thyme and celery salt into the water. Return racks of ribs to seasoned water and set fryer setting to medium. Bring water to a boil. Reduce heat, cover fryer with lid and let water simmer for 1½ hours. Remove ribs from water. Ribs are now ready for additional seasonings and to be placed over indirect heat on grill for 45 minutes. Smother ribs with your favorite BBQ sauce for last 15 minutes of grilling time.

Delicious Prime Rib

Makes 8 to 12 servings

3 to 4 gallons peanut oil   1 tsp. garlic powder
  (see Note 2 on page 1)   2 tsp. onion powder
1 (4 to 6 lb.) boneless   2 tsp. salt
  beef prime rib roast   3 T. Grey Poupon mustard
3 C. dry red wine   3 T. horseradish sauce
1 C. olive oil   3 T. lime juice
2 T. wine vinegar   2 T. cayenne pepper

Add measured amount of peanut oil to a 7 to 10 gallon fryer pot (see Note 2 on page 1). Set fryer to medium-high setting and heat oil to 350°F. It should take about 30+ minutes to heat the oil, depending on the amount of oil, outside temperature and wind conditions.

Meanwhile, wrap prime rib roast completely with plastic wrap. In a blender, combine red wine, olive oil, wine vinegar, garlic powder, onion powder, salt, mustard, horseradish sauce, lime juice and cayenne pepper. Process until liquefied. Using a poultry injector, inject marinade into prime rib, using 1½ to 2 ounces of marinade per pound of meat. Remove plastic wrap and pat prime rib with paper towels until dry. Sprinkle with additional cayenne pepper and salt. Place prime rib on frying rack or in fryer basket.

Lower prime rib into oil (see Note 3 on page 1). Fry roast for 45 minutes to 1 hour (about 10 minutes per pound). When prime rib has been cooked to 160°F, carefully remove from the hot oil and turn off the fryer. Allow prime rib to drain for a few minutes on paper towels. Cover rib roast with aluminum foil and let rest for 10 minutes before carving.

Let hot oil cool completely before transferring to storage containers or disposing (see Note 4 on page 1).

Low Country Boil

Makes 16 servings

Water
4 bags Crab Boil
  mix
4 lbs. whole new
  potatoes
16 pieces short ear
  corn

2 lbs. link sausages,
  precooked
2 lbs. shrimp, shelled
  and deveined
2 lbs. crawfish

Fill turkey fryer pot halfway with water. Set fryer to medium-high setting and bring water to a boil. It should take about 10+ minutes to heat the water. Add Crab Boil mix bags. When water is boiling, add potatoes. After potatoes have been in boiling water for 6 minutes, add corn. After 3 minutes, add precooked sausage links. After an additional 3 minutes, add shrimp and crawfish. Total cook time should be about 27 minutes. To serve, cover picnic table with thick paper or newspaper. Remove fryer basket from turkey fryer and let ingredients drain of water. Pour entire basket of food onto newspaper in middle of table and encourage everyone to eat from the table – Louisiana style!

Crab & Crawfish Boil

Makes 16 to 20 servings

Water
2 lbs. kosher salt
3 lbs. small red potatoes
6 lemons, halved
3 oranges, halved
4 heads garlic, halved
3 large onions, halved
6 packets Zatarain's
   Crab Boil

1 C. Tabasco sauce
½ C. red pepper
   flakes
8 large ears of corn,
   shucked and halved
3 Dungeness crabs,
   cracked and quartered
2 lbs. Gulf shrimp
25 lbs. Louisiana crawfish

Fill turkey fryer pot halfway with water and salt. Set fryer to medium-high setting and bring water to a boil. It should take about 10+ minutes to heat the water. When water is boiling, add fryer basket to fryer. Place potatoes, lemons, oranges, garlic, onions, Crab Boil packets, Tabasco sauce and red pepper flakes in fryer basket. Reduce heat and let mixture simmer for 30 minutes, covered, until potatoes are tender. Add corn and return mixture to a boil. Add crabs, shrimp and crawfish. Cover turkey fryer and turn off the heat. Let seafood steep for about 6 minutes in hot liquid, until fully cooked. Remove fryer basket from turkey fryer and let ingredients drain of water. Pour entire basket of food onto newspaper in middle of table and encourage everyone to eat from the table.

Deep Fried Steak

Makes 4 steaks

3 to 4 gallons peanut oil
(see Note 2 on page 1)
4 steaks of desired
thickness
3 T. coarse salt

3 T. paprika
2 T. pepper
1 T. garlic powder
1 T. onion powder
1 T. dried thyme

Add measured amount of peanut oil to a 7 to 10 gallon fryer pot (see Note 2 on page 1). Set fryer to medium-high setting and heat oil to 350°F. It should take about 30+ minutes to heat the oil, depending on the amount of oil, outside temperature and wind conditions.

Meanwhile, in a medium bowl, combine coarse salt, paprika, pepper, garlic powder, onion powder and dried thyme. Rub seasoning into steaks until thoroughly coated. Place steaks on frying rack or in fryer basket.

Lower steaks into oil (see Note 3 on page 1). Fry steaks according to chart below. When steaks are tender, carefully remove from the hot oil and turn off the fryer. Allow steaks to drain for a few minutes on paper towels.

Let hot oil cool completely before transferring to storage containers or disposing (see Note 4 on page 1).

Thickness	Medium Rare	Medium	Well Done
$\frac{1}{2}$"	1 Minute	2 Minutes	3 Minutes
$\frac{3}{4}$"	2 Minutes	3 Minutes	4 Minutes
1"	3 Minutes	4 Minutes	5 Minutes
$1\frac{1}{4}$"	4 Minutes	5 Minutes	6 Minutes

Canning Summer Vegetables

Canning jars and lids   Boiling water
Water   Various fresh vegetables

If fruits and vegetables are properly canned, the jars will keep oxygen and enzymes from stimulating the growth of bacteria, yeasts and mold. If vegetables are secured in a tightly vacuumed jar, the seal will keep liquid in and harmful air and microorganisms out.

Discard any canning jars or lids that have cracks, chips, dents or rust or defects on the airtight seals. Use pint or quart jars with tight fitting metal sealing lids and metal screw bands. Select desired vegetables to can from chart on the next page. Use only fresh, tender vegetables. The sooner the vegetables are moved from garden to sealed and canned, the better. To prepare vegetables, wash all vegetables thoroughly and handle carefully to avoid bruising.

Fill turkey fryer pot with water and set fryer to medium setting. Place jars in water and bring water to a boil. When water is boiling, reduce heat and carefully remove jars from pot. Place all jar lids in shallow pie dish and pour boiling water over lids. Fill jars with cleaned, fresh vegetables. For corn, peas or lima beans, fill jars to within 1" from the top. For all other vegetables, fill jars to within $\frac{1}{2}$" from the top. Pour boiling water over vegetables in jars. Remove air bubbles by carefully running a spatula along the inside of the jars. Wipe the top of the jar rims with a clean paper towel. Place sealing lids and metal screw bands on top of the jar, screwing as tightly as possible.

(Continued on Next Page)

Return filled jars to turkey fryer pot with hot water. Return water to a boil. Process for required amount of time for vegetables on chart. As soon as the processing time has completed, remove jars from turkey fryer pot. Do not tighten lids. Set jars 2" to 3" apart on clean cloths or wire racks to cool. When jars have cooled completely, about 3 to 4 hours after removing from water, test that the jars have sealed and remove screw bands. Carefully wash off screw bands and filled jars. Dry jars thoroughly and store.

Vegetable	Preparation	Processing Time (For Quart Jars)
Asparagus	Use tender 4" to 6" spears.	40 minutes
Dry Beans or Peas	Use young, thoroughly washed beans.	90 minutes
Whole or Sliced Beets	Cut off tops, leaving 1" of stem.	35 minutes
Carrots	Wash, peel and rewash.	30 minutes
Whole Kernel Corn	Husk corn, remove silk and wash. Cut corn from the cob.	85 minutes
Greens or Spinach	Sort and wash, discard tough stems.	90 minutes
Whole or Sliced Mushrooms	Only high quality. Trim stems and discolored. parts. Soak in cold water for 10 minutes.	45 minutes (pint jars only)
Peppers	Select firm peppers. Wash and drain.	35 minutes (pint jars only)
White Potatoes	Wash and pare.	40 minutes
Sweet Potatoes	Choose small to medium potatoes, wash well.	90 minutes

Poboy Sandwiches

Makes 16 sandwiches

Frying oil
6 lbs. shrimp, peeled
  and deveined
4 eggs
4 tsp. salt
2 tsp. garlic powder
1 tsp. dried oregano
½ tsp. pepper
2 C. flour

4 C. cornmeal
4 (16 oz.) loaves French
  bread, sliced in half
  horizontally
Mayonnaise
Creole mustard
4 C. shredded cabbage
2 ripe tomatoes, thinly
  sliced

Pour frying oil into fryer pot. Set fryer to medium-high setting and heat oil to 375°F. It should take about 30+ minutes to heat the oil, depending on the amount of oil, outside temperature and wind conditions. Meanwhile, rinse shrimp under cool water and pat dry completely. In a medium bowl, combine eggs, salt, garlic powder, dried oregano and pepper, beating until frothy. On two separate large sheets of waxed paper, place flour and cornmeal. Dredge the shrimp in the flour and dip in the egg mixture. Roll shrimp in cornmeal and place on wire racks until all shrimp are coated.

When oil temperature reaches 375° on a deep-fry thermometer, slowly place coated shrimp into the oil.

Fry each batch of shrimp for 1 to 2 minutes or until golden. Remove shrimp from oil with a slotted spoon or using the fryer basket and set on paper towels to drain. To assemble sandwiches, spread inside of French loaves with desired amount of mayonnaise and Creole mustard. Layer sandwiches with shredded cabbage, tomato slices and fried shrimp. Cut each loaf into 4 sandwiches.

Let hot oil cool completely before transferring to storage containers or disposing (see Note 4 on page 1).

Ideas & Recipes for Fall

Homemade Tortilla Chips

Makes 32 servings

Frying oil
2 (25 oz.) pkgs. 8" corn
  tortillas

Salt or Cajun seasoning
Salsa, optional

Pour frying oil into fryer pot. Set fryer to medium-high setting and heat oil to 350°F. It should take about 20+ minutes to heat the oil, depending on the amount of oil, outside temperature and wind conditions. Meanwhile, cut corn tortillas into quarters.

When oil temperature reaches 350° on a deep-fry thermometer, slowly place a handful of cut tortillas into the oil.

Fry each batch of tortilla chips for 1 minute or until golden, turning once. Remove chips from oil and set on paper towels to drain. Sprinkle with salt or Cajun seasoning. If desired, serve warm chips with salsa.

Let hot oil cool completely before transferring to storage containers or disposing (see Note 4 on page 1).

Corn Fritters

Makes about 48 fritters

Frying oil
2 C. flour
2 tsp. baking powder
2 tsp. sugar
1½ tsp. salt
½ tsp. white pepper

4 eggs, separated
1 C. milk
4 T. butter, melted
3 C. fresh, frozen or
   canned whole corn
   kernels

Pour frying oil into fryer pot. Set fryer to medium-high setting and heat oil to 375°F. It should take about 30+ minutes to heat the oil, depending on the amount of oil, outside temperature and wind conditions. Meanwhile, in a medium bowl, combine flour, baking powder, sugar, salt and white pepper. In a small bowl, lightly beat egg yolks, milk and melted butter. Stir butter mixture into flour mixture just until combined. Add corn kernels. In a medium mixing bowl, beat egg whites until stiff peaks form. Fold egg whites into corn mixture.

When oil temperature reaches 375° on a deep-fry thermometer, slowly drop tablespoonfuls of the corn batter into the oil.

Fry fritters for 3 to 4 minutes or until golden. Remove fritters from oil with a slotted spoon or using the fryer basket and set on paper towels to drain.

Let hot oil cool completely before transferring to storage containers or disposing (see Note 4 on page 1).

Hush Puppies

Makes about 30

Frying oil
3 C. cornmeal
3 C. flour
1 C. sugar
2 tsp. baking powder
Pinch of baking soda
Pinch of garlic salt

Salt and pepper to taste
1 (15 oz.) can cream
 style corn
2 large green pepper,
 diced
2 large onions, diced
2 eggs

Pour frying oil into fryer pot. Set fryer to medium-high setting and heat oil to 375°F. It should take about 30+ minutes to heat the oil, depending on the amount of oil, outside temperature and wind conditions. Meanwhile, in a large bowl, combine cornmeal, flour, sugar, baking powder, baking soda, garlic salt, salt, pepper, cream style corn, diced green peppers, diced onions and eggs. Mix until well blended.

When oil temperature reaches 375° on a deep-fry thermometer, slowly drop tablespoonfuls of the batter into the oil.

Fry hush puppies for 4 to 5 minutes or until golden. Remove hush puppies from oil with a slotted spoon or using the fryer basket and set on paper towels to drain.

Let hot oil cool completely before transferring to storage containers or disposing (see Note 4 on page 1).

Onion Mums

Makes 6 onion blossoms

Frying oil
3½ C. flour, divided
6 tsp. paprika, divided
2 tsp. garlic powder
1½ tsp. pepper, divided
¼ tsp. cayenne pepper

⅓ C. cornstarch
2 tsp. garlic salt
1 tsp. salt
6 large Walla Walla
  sweet onions
2 (12 oz.) cans of beer

Pour frying oil into fryer pot. Set fryer to medium-high setting and heat oil to 375°F. It should take about 30+ minutes to heat the oil, depending on the amount of oil, outside temperature and wind conditions. Meanwhile, in a medium bowl, combine 2 cups flour, 4 teaspoons paprika, garlic powder, ½ teaspoon pepper and ¼ teaspoon cayenne pepper. In a large bowl, combine remaining 1½ cups flour, cornstarch, garlic salt, remaining 2 teaspoons paprika, salt, remaining 1 teaspoon pepper and beer. Mix well. Cut onions into quarters from top of onion to within ½" of the base, leaving the base intact. Cut the onion in quarters again and gently spread slices apart to form petals. Cover onions in flour mixture, shaking off excess and dip in batter.

When oil temperature reaches 375° on a deep-fry thermometer, slowly lower battered onions into the oil, petals facing up.

Fry onions for 3 minutes. Remove onions from oil with a slotted spoon and let cool slightly. Carefully spread petals as far apart as possible and lower into hot oil again, petals facing down, and fry for an additional 3 minutes. Remove onions and set on paper towels to drain.

Let hot oil cool completely before transferring to storage containers or disposing (see Note 4 on page 1).

Top Sirloin Chili

Makes 32 servings

½ C. vegetable oil
8 onions, chopped
12 cloves garlic, minced
4 lbs. ground beef
3 lbs. beef sirloin, cubed
4 (14½ oz.) cans diced
   tomatoes in juice
4 (12 oz.) cans dark beer
4 C. strong brewed
   coffee
8 (6 oz.) cans tomato
   paste
4 (14 oz.) cans beef
   broth

2 C. brown sugar
¾ C. chili powder
¼ C. cumin seeds
¼ C. cocoa powder
4 tsp. dried oregano
4 tsp. cayenne pepper
4 tsp. ground coriander
4 tsp. salt
8 (15 oz.) cans kidney
   beans, drained, divided
8 fresh hot chile peppers,
   seeded and chopped

In the turkey fryer pot, place vegetable oil, chopped onions, minced garlic, ground beef and cubed sirloin. Set fryer to low heat and cook for 10 minutes, stirring often with a long spoon, until ground beef and sirloin are fully browned and tender. Mix in diced tomatoes in juice, beer, coffee, tomato paste and beef broth. Add brown sugar, chili powder, cumin seeds, cocoa powder, dried oregano, cayenne pepper, ground coriander and salt. Stir in four cans of the drained kidney beans and chopped chile peppers. Reduce heat to very low, cover pot and let simmer for 1½ hours, stirring frequently. Stir in remaining four cans kidney beans and simmer for an additional 30 minutes.

French Fried Tomatoes

Makes 16 servings

Frying oil	¼ tsp. pepper
8 large ripe tomatoes	2 eggs, lightly beaten
2 tsp. salt	½ C. milk
2 tsp. sugar	2 C. dry bread crumbs

Pour frying oil into fryer pot. Set fryer to medium-high setting and heat oil to 370°F. It should take about 25+ minutes to heat the oil, depending on the amount of oil, outside temperature and wind conditions. Meanwhile, wash tomatoes and cut each tomato into 1" slices. Sprinkle tomato slices with salt, sugar and pepper. In a medium bowl, whisk together eggs and milk. Place dry bread crumbs in a separate bowl. Dip tomatoes slices in egg mixture and then cover with bread crumbs.

When oil temperature reaches 370° on a deep-fry thermometer, slowly place battered tomatoes into the oil.

Fry tomatoes for 1 minute. Remove tomatoes from oil with a slotted spoon or using the fryer basket and set on paper towels to drain.

Let hot oil cool completely before transferring to storage containers or disposing (see Note 4 on page 1).

Pork Tenderloins

Makes 16 servings

3 to 4 gallons peanut oil	2 T. wine vinegar
(see Note 2 on page 1)	1 tsp. garlic powder
4 (1 lb.) pork tenderloins	2 tsp. onion powder
3 C. dry red wine	2 tsp. salt
1 C. olive oil	2 T. cayenne pepper

Add measured amount of peanut oil to a 7 to 10 gallon fryer pot (see Note 2 on page 1). Set fryer to medium-high setting and heat oil 2 to 350°F. It should take about 30+ minutes to heat the oil, depending on the amount of oil, outside temperature and wind conditions.

Meanwhile, wrap pork tenderloins completely with plastic wrap. In a blender, combine red wine, olive oil, wine vinegar, garlic powder, onion powder, salt and cayenne pepper. Mix well until liquefied. Using a poultry injector, inject marinade into tenderloins, using $1\frac{1}{2}$ to 2 ounces of marinade per pound of meat. Remove plastic wrap and pat tenderloins with paper towels until dry. Sprinkle with additional cayenne pepper and salt. Place tenderloins on frying rack or in fryer basket.

Lower tenderloins into oil (see Note 3 on page 1). Fry tenderloins for 48 minutes to 1 hour (about 12 to 15 minutes per pound). When tenderloins are cooked to 160°F, carefully remove from the hot oil and turn off the fryer. Allow tenderloins to drain for a few minutes on paper towels.

Let hot oil cool completely before transferring to storage containers or disposing (see Note 4 on page 1).

Venison Cutlets

Makes 16 servings

16 (4 oz.) venison cutlets	Frying oil
6 C. buttermilk, divided	3 C. flour
4 T. plus 1 tsp. Cajun seasoning	3 C. cornstarch
$\frac{1}{4}$ C. butter, melted	4 tsp. garlic powder
	2 tsp. dry mustard
	4 large eggs

Place venison cutlets between waxed paper and, using a meat mallet, pound meat to $\frac{1}{4}$" thickness. In a medium bowl, combine 4 cups buttermilk, 1 teaspoon Cajun seasoning and melted butter. Place venison cutlets in large plastic bags and pour buttermilk mixture over venison. Seal bags and refrigerate overnight.

Pour frying oil into fryer pot. Set fryer to medium-high setting and heat oil to 350°F. It should take about 20+ minutes to heat the oil, depending on the amount of oil, outside temperature and wind conditions. Meanwhile, drain venison and discard buttermilk mixture. In a large bowl, combine flour, cornstarch, remaining 4 tablespoons Cajun seasoning, garlic powder and dry mustard. In a separate bowl, combine eggs and remaining 2 cups buttermilk. Dredge venison pieces in flour mixture, shaking off excess. Dip venison in batter, shake off excess and dredge again in flour mixture.

When oil temperature reaches 375° on a deep-fry thermometer, slowly lower battered venison into the oil.

Fry cutlets for 2 to 3 minutes. Remove cutlets from oil and set on paper towels to drain.

Let hot oil cool completely before transferring to storage containers or disposing (see Note 4 on page 1).

Apple Fritters

Makes 40 fritters

Frying oil
4 C. flour
½ C. sugar
2 T. baking powder
1 tsp. nutmeg
2 tsp. salt

4 eggs
2 C. milk
8 large apples, peeled
    and cored
Powdered sugar for dusting

Pour frying oil into fryer pot. Set fryer to medium-high setting and heat oil to 375°F. It should take about 30+ minutes to heat the oil, depending on the amount of oil, outside temperature and wind conditions. Meanwhile, in a large bowl, combine flour, sugar, baking powder, nutmeg and salt. In a separate bowl, whisk together eggs and milk. Stir milk mixture into flour mixture until batter is smooth. Slice apples into ½" rings. Dip apple rings in batter mixture, shaking off excess.

When oil temperature reaches 375° on a deep-fry thermometer, slowly place battered apples into the oil.

Fry fritters, turning once, until golden. Remove fritters from oil and set on paper towels to drain. Dust with powdered sugar before serving.

Let hot oil cool completely before transferring to storage containers or disposing (see Note 4 on page 1).

Sopapillas

Makes 48 servings

Frying oil

8 C. flour

4 tsp. baking powder

2 tsp. salt

8 T. shortening

3 C. warm water

Pour frying oil into fryer pot. Set fryer to medium-high setting and heat oil to 375°F. It should take about 30+ minutes to heat the oil, depending on the amount of oil, outside temperature and wind conditions. Meanwhile, in a large bowl, combine flour, baking powder, salt and shortening. Stir in warm water until a smooth dough forms. Cover dough and let stand for 20 minutes. Roll dough out on a lightly floured flat surface to $\frac{1}{4}$" thickness. Cut dough into squares, re-rolling as needed.

When oil temperature reaches 375° on a deep-fry thermometer, slowly place squares into the oil.

Fry sopapillas, turning once, until golden. Remove sopapillas from oil and set on paper towels to drain. Serve warm.

Let hot oil cool completely before transferring to storage containers or disposing (see Note 4 on page 1).

Spiced Apple Cider

Makes 6 gallons

6 gallons apple cider
6 whole cloves
6 cinnamon sticks

2 T. allspice
Butter and brown sugar

In the turkey fryer pot, place apple cider, whole cloves, cinnamon sticks and allspice. Set fryer to low heat and bring mixture to a boil, stirring occasionally. Reduce heat to very low, cover pot and let simmer for 1 to 1½ hours, stirring occasionally. To serve, pour hot spiced cider into mugs and float a small pad of butter and sprinkle of brown sugar on top of each serving.

Home Brewed Beer

1 (10 gallon) food grade
   plastic pail with lid
1 (40 oz.) can malt
   extract
6 to 7 C. sugar
1 tsp. brewer's yeast

Hydrometer
12 (2 liter) plastic bottles
1 (74") tube vinyl
   siphon hose
Hose clamp for siphon

The most important tip to making homemade beer is sanitation. Thoroughly wash all equipment with slightly soapy warm water. Rinse well to remove soap residue and sanitize equipment with a solution of 1 tablespoon bleach dissolved in 1 gallon of water. Pour 10 liters of fresh, cold water into the 10 gallon plastic pail. In the turkey fryer pot, place 7 liters of water. Set fryer to low heat and bring water to a boil. Add malt extract to boiling water, reduce heat to very low and let simmer for 20 minutes. Add sugar and stir, using a long spoon, until sugar is completely dissolved.

(Continued on Next Page)

Quickly pour mixture into pail. Add more water until 10 gallon pail is slightly more than half full. Sprinkle yeast over mixture in pail and stir well. Cover pail loosely with lid. If pail is closed too tightly, the mixture can explode from the carbon dioxide that is produced. Keep pail covered and avoid unnecessary opening. Pail should be stored at a room temperature between 16 to 24°C. The beer will be ready to bottle in 6 to 10 days. Test the readiness of the beer with the hydrometer. Place hydrometer in beer and spin it once. When the hydrometer reads between 1.008 and 1.015, the beer is ready to bottle. There should be little or no bubbling action in the beer. To bottle the beer, place 2 liter bottles over newspaper on the floor. Place about 2 teaspoons sugar in each bottle. Using the siphon hose and the hose clamp, siphon the beer into the bottles, trying not to disturb the sediment on the bottom of the pail. As you near the bottom of the pail, carefully tip the pail. It is important not to agitate or splash the beer too much. Do not fill bottles completely. Tightly screw on bottle caps and invert bottles, shaking to dissolve the sugar in each bottle. For 3 days, store the bottles in a warm area and then move to a dark, cool spot. The beer will improve with age, but is ready to drink after about 1 week of storage.

*Note: plastic bottles should be reused only once, as harmful chemicals can be released within the bottles over time. If available, substitute with glass bottles.

Homemade Maple Syrup

Drill with $\frac{7}{16}$" drill bit
Spouts
Plastic gallon jugs

Candy thermometer
Glass jars

Maple syrup is made from the sap of sugar maple trees. The sap is very thin and watery, but contains about 2 percent sugar. If you boil the sap to remove the water, you will eventually be left with maple syrup. It takes about 30 to 40 gallons of sap to make 1 gallon of maple syrup. To produce sap, the trunk of the sugar maple tree should be at least 10" in diameter. For every additional 8", another hole and spout may be added. For example, a tree that is 26" in diameter could have three holes and spouts. Drill holes with the $\frac{7}{16}$" bit into sugar maple trees and insert spouts into holes. The spout should be inserted tight enough that it cannot be pulled out by hand, but not so tight that it splits the tree bark. Hang the plastic jugs over that hook on the spouts as shown below. When at least 5 gallons of sap have been collected, empty the jugs into the turkey fryer pot. Set fryer to low setting and bring sap to a boil. As the sap boil, more sap can be added. Do not let sap boil below 1" or it may burn. The syrup is done when most of the water has boiled off and the syrup reads 7°F above boiling temperature at your elevation on a candy thermometer. Pour syrup through a strainer into a bucket. Pour syrup back into a large pot and reheat to almost boiling. Pour syrup into glass jars for storage and seal. Store syrup in a cool place until ready to serve.

Ideas & Recipes for Winter

Calzones

Makes 32 calzones

Frying oil
1½ C. shredded
   mozzarella cheese
½ C. finely chopped
   Genoa salami
¼ C. grated Romano
   cheese

2 tsp. dried basil
2 egg yolks
2 (10 oz.) tubes
   refrigerated pizza
   dough
Spaghetti sauce

Pour frying oil into fryer pot. Set fryer to medium-high setting and heat oil to 350°F. It should take about 20+ minutes to heat the oil, depending on the amount of oil, outside temperature and wind conditions. Meanwhile, in a medium bowl, combine mozzarella cheese, chopped salami, Romano cheese, dried basil and egg yolks. Mix until well combined. Unroll pizza dough on a lightly floured flat surface. Roll dough into two 12" squares, evening the edges with a ruler. Cut each square into sixteen 3" squares. Place 1½ teaspoons of the cheese mixture in the center of each square. Brush the edges of the squares lightly with water and fold squares over filling to make a triangle, pressing down on edges to seal. Press down on edges with a fork to securely enclose the filling.

When oil temperature reaches 375° on a deep-fry thermometer, slowly place filled calzones into the oil.

Fry calzones for 3 to 4 minutes, turning once, until golden brown. Remove calzones from oil with a slotted spoon or using the fryer basket and set on paper towels to drain. Serve with spaghetti sauce for dipping.

Let hot oil cool completely before transferring to storage containers or disposing (see Note 4 on page 1).

Crab Rangoons

Makes 48 rangoons

Frying oil
1 (8 oz.) pkg. cream
  cheese, softened
8 oz. fresh or canned
  crab meat, drained
  and flaked
1 tsp. chopped red onion
$\frac{1}{2}$ tsp. Worcestershire
  sauce

$\frac{1}{2}$ tsp. soy sauce
Pepper to taste
1 green onion, finely sliced
1 clove garlic, minced
1 (10 oz.) pkg. wonton
  wrappers

Pour frying oil into fryer pot. Set fryer to medium-high setting and heat oil to 375°F. It should take about 30+ minutes to heat the oil, depending on the amount of oil, outside temperature and wind conditions. Meanwhile, in a medium bowl, combine cream cheese and flaked crabmeat. Mix in chopped red onions, Worcestershire sauce, soy sauce, pepper, sliced green onions and minced garlic. Lay wonton wrappers on a flat surface. Place 1 teaspoon of the cream cheese mixture in the center of each wonton. Brush the edges of the squares lightly with water and fold squares over filling to make a triangle, pressing down on edges to seal. Fold corners in to make a wonton shape.

When oil temperature reaches 375° on a deep-fry thermometer, slowly place filled wontons into the oil.

Fry crab rangoons for about 3 minutes, until golden brown. Remove rangoons from oil with a slotted spoon or using the fryer basket and set on paper towels to drain.

Let hot oil cool completely before transferring to storage containers or disposing (see Note 4 on page 1).

Fried Oysters

Makes 16 servings

Frying oil
6 C. flour
2 C. corn flour

¼ C. Cajun seasoning
4 pints oyster in liquid,
shucked

Pour frying oil into fryer pot. Set fryer to medium-high setting and heat oil to 350°F. It should take about 20+ minutes to heat the oil, depending on the amount of oil, outside temperature and wind conditions. Meanwhile, in a medium bowl, combine flour, corn flour and Cajun seasoning. Dip wet oysters in flour mixture until fully coated.

When oil temperature reaches 375° on a deep-fry thermometer, slowly place coated oysters into the oil.

Fry oysters for about 2 minutes, turning once. Remove oysters from oil with a slotted spoon or using the fryer basket and set on paper towels to drain.

Let hot oil cool completely before transferring to storage containers or disposing (see Note 4 on page 1).

Calamari

Makes 24 servings

Frying oil
2 C. cornmeal
2 C. flour

4 lbs. fresh or frozen
    squid, cut into
    $\frac{1}{2}$" rings

Pour frying oil into fryer pot. Set fryer to medium-high setting and heat oil to 375°F. It should take about 30+ minutes to heat the oil, depending on the amount of oil, outside temperature and wind conditions. Meanwhile, in a large bowl, combine cornmeal and flour. Rinse squid pieces and pat dry thoroughly with paper towels. Add squid pieces to flour mixture and toss until fully coated.

When oil temperature reaches 375° on a deep-fry thermometer, slowly place coated squid into the oil.

Fry squid for about 3 minutes, until golden brown. Remove calamari from oil with a slotted spoon or using the fryer basket and set on paper towels to drain.

Let hot oil cool completely before transferring to storage containers or disposing (see Note 4 on page 1).

Concord Grape Wine

Makes about 1½ gallons

Wine fermenter	5 lbs. sugar
10 lbs. Concord grapes	1 tsp. yeast nutrient
1 gallon water	Wine yeast

The most important tip to making homemade wine is sanitation. Thoroughly wash all equipment with slightly soapy warm water. Rinse well to remove soap residue and sanitize equipment with a solution of 1 tablespoon bleach dissolved in 1 gallon of water. Pull grapes from stems and place grapes in fermenter and crush the grapes. Fill the turkey fryer pot with 1 gallon water. Set fryer to low heat and bring water to a boil. Add sugar and stir, using a long spoon, until sugar is completely dissolved. Pour boiling water mixture over grapes in fermenter. Let mixture cool to room temperature and stir in yeast nutrient and yeast. Let mixture stand for 24 hours. Ferment wine for 2 weeks, stirring daily. Strain wine through a fine sieve into secondary fermenter and let stand for 1 month. At the end of the month, the wine should be clear. Rack wine and let stand for 2 months. After two months, the wine should be ready to bottle.

Glogg

Makes 24 servings

2 (750 ml.) bottles
red wine
4 T. dried orange peel
4 cinnamon sticks
20 whole cardamom
seeds

25 whole cloves
1 lb. blanched almonds
1 lb. raisins
1 lb. sugar cubes
½ C. plus 2 T. brandy

Pour red wine into turkey fryer pot. Set fryer to low setting. In cheesecloth, wrap orange peel, cinnamon sticks, cardamom seeds and cloves and tie with kitchen string. Place filled cheesecloth bag in fryer pot. Bring mixture to a boil for 15 minutes, stirring occasionally. Stir in almonds and raisins and boil for an additional 15 minutes. Remove pot from heat. Place a wire grill over fryer pot and place sugar cubes on grill. Pour the brandy slowly over the sugar cubes, making sure to completely saturate the sugar. With a match, light sugar cubes and let flame. When sugar has melted, cover pot with lid to extinguish flame. Remove spice bag and stir. Serve hot in mugs garnished with a few almonds and raisins.

Deep Fried Ham

Makes about 15 servings

1 C. ketchup
¼ C. honey
¼ C. prepared mustard
1 (7 to 8 lb.) whole
   boneless ham

3 to 4 gallons peanut oil
   (see Note 2 on page 1)

In a small bowl, combine ketchup, honey and mustard. Whisk together until fully blended.

Using paper towels, thoroughly dry outside of ham. Place ham in a large roasting pan or bowl and, using a poultry injector, season the ham by injecting marinade into ham all around outer surface. Cover roasting pan and place overnight in refrigerator.

Add measured amount of peanut oil to a 7 to 10 gallon fryer pot (see Note 2 on page 1). Set fryer to medium-high setting and heat oil to 375°F. It should take about 40+ minutes to heat the oil, depending on the amount of oil, outside temperature and wind conditions. Meanwhile, place ham in the turkey fryer basket or on the rack.

When oil temperature reaches 375° on a deep-fry thermometer, slowly lower ham into the oil. Immediately check the oil temperature and increase the flame so the oil temperature is maintained at 350°. Fry ham for about 3½ minutes per pound, or until ham registers at 170°F on a meat thermometer. Remove ham from rack and place on a serving platter.

Let hot oil cool completely before transferring to storage containers or disposing (see Note 4 on page 1).

French Toast

Makes 16 to 20 servings

Frying oil
4 (13 oz.) loaves French bread
16 eggs

1 C. sugar
¼ C. milk
¼ C. vanilla
Powdered sugar for dusting

Pour frying oil into fryer pot. Set fryer to medium-high setting and heat oil to 350°F. It should take about 20+ minutes to heat the oil, depending on the amount of oil, outside temperature and wind conditions. Meanwhile, cut bread into 1" thick slices. In a large bowl, whisk together eggs, sugar, milk and vanilla. Dip slices into the egg mixture until fully saturated.

When oil temperature reaches 350° on a deep-fry thermometer, slowly place bread slices into the oil.

Fry French toast for about 3 minutes, until golden brown. Remove French toast from oil with a pair of long tongs and set on paper towels to drain. Dust with powdered sugar before serving.

Let hot oil cool completely before transferring to storage containers or disposing (see Note 4 on page 1).

Fried Chicken

Frying oil
3 whole chickens
3 T. Lawry's seasoned
   salt

6 cloves garlic, minced
3 C. flour

Pour frying oil into fryer pot. Set fryer to medium-high setting and heat oil to 375°F. It should take about 30+ minutes to heat the oil, depending on the amount of oil, outside temperature and wind conditions. Meanwhile, divide chickens into drumsticks, wings and breast pieces. In a medium bowl, combine seasoned salt and minced garlic. In a separate bowl, place flour. Roll chicken pieces in garlic mixture and then in flour. Shake off excess flour and roll again in seasonings.

When oil temperature reaches 375° on a deep-fry thermometer, slowly place covered chicken pieces into the oil.

Fry chicken until golden brown. Remove chicken from oil with a slotted spoon or using the fryer basket and set on paper towels to drain.

Let hot oil cool completely before transferring to storage containers or disposing (see Note 4 on page 1).

Spicy Fried Chicken

Makes 16 servings

Frying oil
4 (3 lb.) whole chickens
2 qts. buttermilk
$\frac{1}{4}$ C. Tabasco sauce
7 tsp. cumin, divided

3 T. pepper, divided
4 tsp. cayenne pepper,
  divided
6 C. flour

Pour frying oil into fryer pot. Set fryer to medium-high setting and heat oil to 350°F. It should take about 20+ minutes to heat the oil, depending on the amount of oil, outside temperature and wind conditions. Meanwhile, divide chickens into drumsticks, wings and breast pieces. In a medium bowl, combine buttermilk, Tabasco sauce, $3\frac{1}{2}$ teaspoons cumin, $1\frac{1}{2}$ tablespoons pepper and 2 teaspoons cayenne pepper, whisking until smooth. In a separate bowl, combine flour and remaining $3\frac{1}{2}$ teaspoons cumin, remaining $1\frac{1}{2}$ tablespoons pepper and remaining 2 teaspoons cayenne pepper. Dip chicken pieces in buttermilk mixture and then coat in flour mixture. Shake off excess flour and roll again in flour mixture.

When oil temperature reaches 350° on a deep-fry thermometer, slowly place coated chicken pieces into the oil.

Fry chicken until golden brown. Remove chicken from oil with a slotted spoon or using the fryer basket and set on paper towels to drain.

Let hot oil cool completely before transferring to storage containers or disposing (see Note 4 on page 1).

Southern Fried Chicken

Makes 16 servings

Frying oil
4 (3 lb.) whole chickens
6 T. salt, divided
2 C. flour

3 tsp. pepper
3 tsp. cayenne pepper
2 tsp. dried thyme

Divide chickens into drumsticks, wings and breast pieces. In a large bowl, place chicken pieces and sprinkle with 4 tablespoons salt. Cover chicken with water and refrigerate at least 2 hours.

Pour frying oil into fryer pot. Set fryer to medium-high setting and heat oil to 360°F. It should take about 25+ minutes to heat the oil, depending on the amount of oil, outside temperature and wind conditions. Meanwhile, drain chicken. In a medium bowl, combine flour, pepper, cayenne pepper, dried thyme and remaining 2 tablespoons salt. Dip chicken pieces in flour mixture until well coated.

When oil temperature reaches 350° on a deep-fry thermometer, slowly place coated chicken pieces into the oil.

Fry chicken until golden brown. Remove chicken from oil with a slotted spoon or using the fryer basket and set on paper towels to drain.

Let hot oil cool completely before transferring to storage containers or disposing (see Note 4 on page 1).

Stuffed Pork Chops

Makes 16 servings

Frying oil
16 (8 oz.) pork chops
1 lb. ground Italian
   sausage
2 C. finely chopped onions
2 C. dry bread crumbs

6 C. flour
2 C. cornstarch
2 T. garlic salt
4 eggs
3 C. milk

Pour frying oil into fryer pot. Set fryer to medium-high setting and heat oil to 350°F. It should take about 20+ minutes to heat the oil, depending on the amount of oil, outside temperature and wind conditions. Meanwhile, make $1\frac{1}{2}$" slits in the side of each pork chop on the side opposite the bone, being careful not to slice all the way through the chops. In a medium bowl, combine ground sausage, chopped onions and bread crumbs. Stuff sausage mixture into the slits inside pork chops until all is used. Close chops with wooden toothpicks. In a large bowl, combine flour, cornstarch and garlic salt. In a separate bowl, combine eggs and milk. Dredge stuffed chops in flour mixture and dip into egg mixture. Dredge again in flour mixture.

When oil temperature reaches 350° on a deep-fry thermometer, slowly place stuffed pork chops into the oil.

Fry pork chops until golden brown. Remove pork chops from oil with a pair of long tongs and set on paper towels to drain.

Let hot oil cool completely before transferring to storage containers or disposing (see Note 4 on page 1).

Lobster Boil

Makes 2 lobsters

2 whole live lobsters   **Salt**
Water   **Juice of 3 to 4 lemons**

Fill the fryer pot of the turkey fryer with enough water to cover both lobsters. Set fryer to medium setting and bring water to a boil. Lightly salt the water and add lemon juice. When water is fully boiling, add live lobsters, headfirst, into the water. Return water to a boil and reduce heat to low. Cover fryer pot with lid and let simmer for 5 minutes for the first pound. Cook lobsters for an additional 3 minutes per extra pound. Remove lobsters from water as soon as they are fully cooked and serve. Twist off each large claw. Remove claw meat by cracking with nutcracker. Hold the body of the cooked lobster with a towel and twist of the tails. Remove tail meat by separating the tail shell with fingers.

Sweet Potato Chimichangas

Makes 32 servings

Frying oil
1 (40 oz.) can mashed
  sweet potatoes
1 T. plus 1½ tsp.
  cinnamon, divided
1 (10 oz.) pkg. miniature
  marshmallows

1 T. frozen whipped
  topping, thawed
½ C. powdered sugar
⅓ C. flour
16 (10") flour tortillas
¼ C. butter, softened
1 T. sugar

Pour frying oil into fryer pot. Set fryer to medium-high setting and heat oil to 350°F. It should take about 20+ minutes to heat the oil, depending on the amount of oil, outside temperature and wind conditions. Meanwhile, in a large saucepan over medium heat, combine sweet potatoes and 1 tablespoon cinnamon. Cook until most of the juice has evaporated and stir in marshmallows until almost melted. Remove from heat and let cool. When cool, stir in whipped topping, powdered sugar and flour. Cut tortillas in half and spread a thin layer of butter over one side of each tortilla half. Spread about 1 tablespoon of the potato filling onto each tortilla half. Fold up the sides and roll the tortilla halves to enclose the filling.

When oil temperature reaches 350° on a deep-fry thermometer, slowly place filled tortillas into the oil.

Fry tortillas until golden brown. Remove chimichangas from oil with a slotted spoon or using the fryer basket and set on paper towels to drain.

Let hot oil cool completely before transferring to storage containers or disposing (see Note 4 on page 1).

Cinnamon Cubes

Makes 16 servings

Frying oil	4 tsp. vanilla
16 C. French bread cubes	1⅓ C. flour
4 C. milk	2 C. sugar
4 eggs	2 T. cinnamon

Pour frying oil into fryer pot. Set fryer to medium-high setting and heat oil to 350°F. It should take about 20+ minutes to heat the oil, depending on the amount of oil, outside temperature and wind conditions. Meanwhile, place bread cubes in a single layer in two 9 x 13" baking dishes. In a medium bowl, whisk together milk, eggs and vanilla. Pour mixture over bread cubes and let sit until bread has absorbed the liquid. Remove bread cubes from dishes and set on paper towels. Pat bread cubes lightly to remove excess liquid. Place flour in a large bowl. Toss bread cubes in flour until fully coated, shaking off excess flour.

When oil temperature reaches 350° on a deep-fry thermometer, slowly place breaded cubes into the oil.

Fry bread cubes until golden brown. Remove bread cubes from oil with a slotted spoon or using the fryer basket and set on paper towels to drain. In a large bowl, combine sugar and cinnamon. Mix well. Add drained bread cubes to cinnamon mixture and toss until coated.

Let hot oil cool completely before transferring to storage containers or disposing (see Note 4 on page 1).

Yummy
Turkey
Recipes

The Original

Makes 12 servings

½ (16 oz.) bottle
   Italian dressing
2 T. Worcestershire
   sauce
Hot sauce to taste
¼ C. salt
2 T. pepper
1 T. cayenne pepper

1 T. onion powder
1 T. garlic powder
1 T. celery salt
½ C. water
1 (10 to 12 lb.) whole
   turkey, non self-basting
4 to 5 gallons peanut oil
   (see Note 2 on page 1)

In a blender or food processor, combine Italian dressing, Worcestershire sauce, hot sauce, salt, pepper, cayenne pepper, onion powder, garlic powder, celery salt and water. Blend for 2 to 3 minutes, until seasonings are liquefied.

Remove any plastic bags or pop-up timer from turkey. Remove giblets and neck from turkey and rinse turkey in cold water. Using paper towels, thoroughly dry both outside and inside cavity of turkey. Place turkey in a large roasting pan and, using a poultry injector, season the turkey by injecting marinade 2 to 3 times on each side of the breast and upper thighs. Cut the wing tips from the turkey, as well as small tail, as they may get caught in the fryer basket. If desired, inject any additional marinade into meaty parts of turkey.

Add measured amount of peanut oil to a 7 to 10 gallon fryer pot (see Note 2 on page 1). Set fryer to medium-high setting and heat oil to 375°F. It should take about 40+ minutes to heat the oil, depending on the amount of oil, outside temperature and wind conditions. Meanwhile, place turkey, neck down, in the turkey fryer basket or on the rack.

(Continued on Next Page)

When oil temperature reaches 375° on a deep-fry thermometer, slowly lower turkey into the oil (see Note 3 on page 1). Because of frothing caused by the moisture fro3m the turkey, the level of the oil will rise but will stabilize in about 1 minute.

Immediately check the oil temperature and increase the flame so the oil temperature is maintained at 350°. If the oil temperature drops to 340° or below, oil will begin to seep into the turkey.

Fry turkey for about 3 to 4 minutes per pound, or about 35 to 42 minutes for a 10 to 12 pound turkey. Be sure to stay near the cooker, as the heat must be closely regulated. Using a meat thermometer, check the temperature of the breast or thigh. When the breast has been cooked to 170°F or the thigh has been cooked to 180°F, carefully remove the turkey from the hot oil and turn off the fryer. Allow the turkey to drain for a few minutes. Remove turkey from rack and place on a serving platter. Allow turkey to rest for about 20 minutes before carving.

Let hot oil cool completely before transferring to storage containers or disposing (see Note 4 on page 1).

Cajun Deep-Fried Turkey

Makes 12 servings

½ C. kosher salt
3 T. onion powder
3 T. pepper
3 T. white pepper
2 T. sweet basil
2 tsp. ground bay leaves
1 T. cayenne pepper

2 tsp. file powder
3 T. garlic powder
1½ T. paprika
1 (10 to 12 lb.) whole
  turkey, non self-basting
4 to 5 gallons peanut oil
  (see Note 2 on page 1)

In a small bowl, combine salt, onion powder, pepper, white pepper, sweet basil, ground bay leaves, cayenne pepper, file powder, garlic powder and paprika. Mix until well blended. For a 10 to 12 pound turkey, use ½ to ⅔ cup of the mixture as a rub. The remaining rub can be store in an airtight jar for several months.

Remove any plastic bags or pop-up timer from turkey. Remove giblets and neck from turkey and rinse turkey in cold water. Using paper towels, thoroughly dry both outside and inside cavity of turkey. Place turkey in a large roasting pan and rub with seasoning both inside and outside of turkey. Cut the wing tips from the turkey, as well as small tail, as they may get caught in the fryer basket. Cover roasting pan and place in refrigerator overnight.

Add measured amount of peanut oil to a 7 to 10 gallon fryer pot (see Note 2 on page 1). Set fryer to medium-high setting and heat oil to 375°F. It should take about 40+ minutes to heat the oil, depending on the amount of oil, outside temperature and wind conditions. Meanwhile, place turkey, neck down, in the turkey fryer basket or on the rack.

(Continued on Next Page)

When oil temperature reaches 375° on a deep-fry thermometer, slowly lower turkey into the oil (see Note 3 on page 1). Because of frothing caused by the moisture from the turkey, the level of the oil will rise but will stabilize in about 1 minute.

Immediately check the oil temperature and increase the flame so the oil temperature is maintained at 350°. If the oil temperature drops to 340° or below, oil will begin to seep into the turkey.

Fry turkey for about 3 to 4 minutes per pound, or about 35 to 42 minutes for a 10 to 12 pound turkey. Be sure to stay near the cooker, as the heat must be closely regulated. Using a meat thermometer, check the temperature of the breast or thigh. When the breast has been cooked to 170°F or the thigh has been cooked to 180°F, carefully remove the turkey from the hot oil and turn off the fryer. Allow the turkey to drain for a few minutes. Remove turkey from rack and place on a serving platter. Allow turkey to rest for about 20 minutes before carving.

Let hot oil cool completely before transferring to storage containers or disposing (see Note 4 on page 1).

Southern Deep-Fried Turkey

Makes 12 servings

⅔ C. vinaigrette
   dressing
⅓ C. dry sherry
2 tsp. lemon pepper
   seasoning salt
1 tsp. garlic powder

1 tsp. onion powder
1 tsp. cayenne pepper
1 (10 to 12 lb.) whole
   turkey, non self-basting
4 to 5 gallons peanut oil
   (see Note 2 on page 1)

In a small bowl, combine vinaigrette, dry sherry, lemon pepper seasoning salt, garlic powder, onion powder and cayenne pepper. Mix until well blended and strain marinade through a fine-hole sieve or cheesecloth.

Remove any plastic bags or pop-up timer from turkey. Remove giblets and neck from turkey and rinse turkey in cold water. Using paper towels, thoroughly dry both outside and inside cavity of turkey. Place turkey in a large roasting pan and, using a poultry injector, season the turkey by injecting marinade 2 to 3 times on each side of the breast and upper thighs. Cut the wing tips from the turkey, as well as small tail, as they may get caught in the fryer basket. If desired, inject any additional marinade into meaty parts of turkey.

Add measured amount of peanut oil to a 7 to 10 gallon fryer pot (see Note 2 on page 1). Set fryer to medium-high setting and heat oil to 375°F. It should take about 40+ minutes to heat the oil, depending on the amount of oil, outside temperature and wind conditions. Meanwhile, place turkey, neck down, in the turkey fryer basket or on the rack.

(Continued on Next Page)

When oil temperature reaches 375° on a deep-fry thermometer, slowly lower turkey into the oil (see Note 3 on page 1). Because of frothing caused by the moisture from the turkey, the level of the oil will rise but will stabilize in about 1 minute.

Immediately check the oil temperature and increase the flame so the oil temperature is maintained at 350°. If the oil temperature drops to 340° or below, oil will begin to seep into the turkey.

Fry turkey for about 3 to 4 minutes per pound, or about 35 to 42 minutes for a 10 to 12 pound turkey. Be sure to stay near the cooker, as the heat must be closely regulated. Using a meat thermometer, check the temperature of the breast or thigh. When the breast has been cooked to 170°F or the thigh has been cooked to 180°F, carefully remove the turkey from the hot oil and turn off the fryer. Allow the turkey to drain for a few minutes. Remove turkey from rack and place on a serving platter. Allow turkey to rest for about 20 minutes before carving.

Let hot oil cool completely before transferring to storage containers or disposing (see Note 4 on page 1).

Ginger & Rosemary Deep-Fried Turkey

Makes 12 servings

¼ C. fresh minced
garlic
2 T. kosher salt
2 tsp. pepper
¼ C. fresh gingerroot,
peeled and sliced
2 T. fresh rosemary,
crushed

6 cloves garlic, peeled
1 (10 to 12 lb.) whole
turkey, non self-basting
4 to 5 gallons peanut oil
(see Note 2 on page 1)

In a small bowl, combine minced garlic, salt and pepper. Mix until well blended.

Remove any plastic bags or pop-up timer from turkey. Remove giblets and neck from turkey and rinse turkey in cold water. Using paper towels, thoroughly dry both outside and inside cavity of turkey. Fill cavity of turkey with sliced gingerroot, crushed rosemary and garlic cloves. Place turkey in a large roasting pan and rub minced garlic seasoning over both inside and outside of turkey. Cut the wing tips from the turkey, as well as small tail, as they may get caught in the fryer basket. Cover roasting pan and place in refrigerator for 1 hour.

Meanwhile, add measured amount of peanut oil to a 7 to 10 gallon fryer pot (see Note 2 on page 1). Set fryer to medium-high setting and heat oil to 375°F. It should take about 40+ minutes to heat the oil, depending on the amount of oil, outside temperature and wind conditions. After chilling in refrigerator for 1 hour, remove ginger, rosemary and garlic from turkey cavity and place turkey, neck down, in the turkey fryer basket or on the rack.

(Continued on Next Page)

When oil temperature reaches 375° on a deep-fry thermometer, slowly lower turkey into the oil (see Note 3 on page 1). Because of frothing caused by the moisture from the turkey, the level of the oil will rise but will stabilize in about 1 minute.

Immediately check the oil temperature and increase the flame so the oil temperature is maintained at 350°. If the oil temperature drops to 340° or below, oil will begin to seep into the turkey.

Fry turkey for about 3 to 4 minutes per pound, or about 35 to 42 minutes for a 10 to 12 pound turkey. Be sure to stay near the cooker, as the heat must be closely regulated. Using a meat thermometer, check the temperature of the breast or thigh. When the breast has been cooked to 170°F or the thigh has been cooked to 180°F, carefully remove the turkey from the hot oil and turn off the fryer. Allow the turkey to drain for a few minutes. Remove turkey from rack and place on a serving platter. Allow turkey to rest for about 20 minutes before carving.

Let hot oil cool completely before transferring to storage containers or disposing (see Note 4 on page 1).

Spicy Italian Deep-Fried Turkey

Makes 12 servings

1 C. Italian dressing, strained
1 C. white wine
1 (26 oz.) box free-flowing salt
3 T. pepper
¼ C. cayenne pepper
2 T. garlic powder
2 T. chili powder
1 (10 to 12 lb.) whole turkey, non self-basting
4 to 5 gallons peanut oil (see Note 2 on page 1)

In a small bowl, combine strained Italian dressing and white wine. In a separate bowl, combine salt, pepper, cayenne pepper, garlic powder and chili powder. Mix until well blended and sprinkle half of the salt mixture over the Italian dressing mixture. Stir thoroughly and constantly so the dressing and wine do not separate.

Remove any plastic bags or pop-up timer from turkey. Remove giblets and neck from turkey and rinse turkey in cold water. Using paper towels, thoroughly dry both outside and inside cavity of turkey. Place turkey in a large roasting pan and, using a poultry injector, season the turkey by injecting marinade 2 to 3 times on each side of the breast and upper thighs. Cut the wing tips from the turkey, as well as small tail, as they may get caught in the fryer basket. If desired, inject any additional marinade into meaty parts of turkey. Rub remaining half of the salt mixture over the outside and inside cavity of turkey. Cover roasting pan and turkey with a plastic bag and place overnight in refrigerator.

(Continued on Next Page)

Add measured amount of peanut oil to a 7 to 10 gallon fryer pot (see Note 2 on page 1). Set fryer to medium-high setting and heat oil to 375°F. It should take about 40+ minutes to heat the oil, depending on the amount of oil, outside temperature and wind conditions. Meanwhile, place turkey, neck down, in the turkey fryer basket or on the rack.

When oil temperature reaches 375° on a deep-fry thermometer, slowly lower turkey into the oil (see Note 3 on page 1). Because of frothing caused by the moisture from the turkey, the level of the oil will rise but will stabilize in about 1 minute.

Immediately check the oil temperature and increase the flame so the oil temperature is maintained at 350°. If the oil temperature drops to 340° or below, oil will begin to seep into the turkey.

Fry turkey for about 3 to 4 minutes per pound, or about 35 to 42 minutes for a 10 to 12 pound turkey. Be sure to stay near the cooker, as the heat must be closely regulated. Using a meat thermometer, check the temperature of the breast or thigh. When the breast has been cooked to 170°F or the thigh has been cooked to 180°F, carefully remove the turkey from the hot oil and turn off the fryer. Allow the turkey to drain for a few minutes. Remove turkey from rack and place on a serving platter. Allow turkey to rest for about 20 minutes before carving.

Let hot oil cool completely before transferring to storage containers or disposing (see Note 4 on page 1).

Louisiana Fried Turkey Breast

Makes 6 servings

1 T. kosher salt
¼ tsp. pepper
1 T. onion powder
1½ tsp. garlic powder
1 tsp. cayenne pepper

1 (3½ to 4 lb.) turkey
  breast, non self-basting
2 to 3 gallons peanut oil
  (see Note 2 on page 1)

In a small bowl, combine kosher salt, pepper, onion powder, garlic powder and cayenne pepper. Stir until seasonings are fully combined.

Rinse turkey breast completely in cold water. Using paper towels, thoroughly dry both outside and inside of turkey breast. Rub seasoning mixture to coat all surfaces of the turkey breast. Place turkey breast in the turkey fryer basket or on the rack, neck side down.

Add measured amount of peanut oil to a 7 to 10 gallon fryer pot (see Note 2 on page 1). Set fryer to medium-high setting and heat oil to 375°F. It should take about 30+ minutes to heat the oil, depending on the amount of oil, outside temperature and wind conditions.

When oil temperature reaches 375° on a deep-fry thermometer, slowly lower turkey breast into the oil (see Note 3 on page 1). Because of frothing caused by the moisture from the turkey breast, the level of the oil will rise but will stabilize in about 1 minute.

(Continued on Next Page)

Immediately check the oil temperature and increase the flame so the oil temperature is maintained at 350°. If the oil temperature drops to 340° or below, oil will begin to seep into the turkey.

Fry turkey for about 4 to 5 minutes per pound, or about 15 to 20 minutes for a $3\frac{1}{2}$ to 4 pound turkey breast. Be sure to stay near the cooker, as the heat must be closely regulated. Using a meat thermometer, check the temperature of the breast. When the breast has been cooked to 170°F, carefully remove the turkey breast from the hot oil and turn off the fryer. Allow the breast to drain for a few minutes. Remove turkey breast from rack and place on a serving platter. Allow turkey breast to rest for about 15 minutes before carving.

Let hot oil cool completely before transferring to storage containers or disposing (see Note 4 on page 1).

Deep-Fried Turkey Made-Easy

Makes 12 servings

1 (10 to 12 lb.) whole turkey, non self-basting	Salt
	Lemon juice
	Hot pepper sauce
4 to 5 gallons peanut oil (see Note 2 on page 1)	Lemon wedges for garnish

Remove any plastic bags or pop-up timer from turkey. Remove giblets and neck from turkey and rinse turkey in cold water. Using paper towels, thoroughly dry both outside and inside cavity of turkey. Cut the wing tips from the turkey, as well as small tail, as they may get caught in the fryer basket.

Add measured amount of peanut oil to a 7 to 10 gallon fryer pot (see Note 2 on page 1). Set fryer to medium-high setting and heat oil 2 to 375°F. It should take about 40+ minutes to heat the oil, depending on the amount of oil, outside temperature and wind conditions. Meanwhile, place turkey, neck down, in the turkey fryer basket or on the rack.

When oil temperature reaches 375° on a deep-fry thermometer, slowly lower turkey into the oil (see Note 3 on page 1). Because of frothing caused by the moisture from the turkey, the level of the oil will rise but will stabilize in about 1 minute.

Immediately check the oil temperature and increase the flame so the oil temperature is maintained at 350°. If the oil temperature drops to 340° or below, oil will begin to seep into the turkey.

(Continued on Next Page)

Fry turkey for about 3 to 4 minutes per pound, or about 35 to 42 minutes for a 10 to 12 pound turkey. Be sure to stay near the cooker, as the heat must be closely regulated. Using a meat thermometer, check the temperature of the breast or thigh. When the breast has been cooked to 170°F or the thigh has been cooked to 180°F, carefully remove the turkey from the hot oil and turn off the fryer. Allow the turkey to drain for a few minutes. Remove turkey from rack and place on a serving platter. Allow turkey to rest for about 20 minutes before carving.

After carving, sprinkle turkey generously with salt and lemon juice. Serve with hot pepper sauce on the side. Garnish with fresh lemon wedges.

Let hot oil cool completely before transferring to storage containers or disposing (see Note 4 on page 1).

Double Spicy Deep-Fried Turkey

Makes 12 servings

½ C. liquid garlic
½ C. liquid onion
½ C. liquid celery
1 T. cayenne pepper
2 T. salt
2 T. Tabasco sauce

2 T. liquid crab boil or
   1 tsp. Old Bay seasoning
1 (10 to 12 lb.) turkey,
   non self-basting
4 to 5 gallons peanut oil
   (see Note 2 on page 1)

To make marinade, in a medium frying pan over medium high heat, combine liquid garlic, liquid onion, liquid celery, cayenne pepper, salt, Tabasco sauce and Old Bay seasoning. Sauté ingredients until cayenne pepper and salt are completely dissolved.

Remove any plastic bags or pop-up timer from turkey. Remove giblets and neck from turkey and rinse turkey in cold water. Using paper towels, thoroughly dry both outside and inside cavity of turkey. Place turkey in a large roasting pan and, using a poultry injector, season the turkey by injecting marinade 2 to 3 times on each side of the breast and upper thighs. Cut the wing tips from the turkey, as well as small tail, as they may get caught in the fryer basket. If desired, inject any additional marinade into meaty parts of turkey.

Add measured amount of peanut oil to a 7 to 10 gallon fryer pot (see Note 2 on page 1). Set fryer to medium-high setting and heat oil to 375°F. It should take about 40+ minutes to heat the oil, depending on the amount of oil, outside temperature and wind conditions. Meanwhile, place turkey, neck down, in the turkey fryer basket or on the rack.

(Continued on Next Page)

When oil temperature reaches 375° on a deep-fry thermometer, slowly lower turkey into the oil (see Note 3 on page 1). Because of frothing caused by the moisture from the turkey, the level of the oil will rise but will stabilize in about 1 minute.

Immediately check the oil temperature and increase the flame so the oil temperature is maintained at 350°. If the oil temperature drops to 340° or below, oil will begin to seep into the turkey.

Fry turkey for about 3 to 4 minutes per pound, or about 35 to 42 minutes for a 10 to 12 pound turkey. Be sure to stay near the cooker, as the heat must be closely regulated. Using a meat thermometer, check the temperature of the breast or thigh. When the breast has been cooked to 170°F or the thigh has been cooked to 180°F, carefully remove the turkey from the hot oil and turn off the fryer. Allow the turkey to drain for a few minutes. Remove turkey from rack and place on a serving platter. Allow turkey to rest for about 20 minutes before carving.

Let hot oil cool completely before transferring to storage containers or disposing (see Note 4 on page 1).

Maple Pecan Glazed Deep-Fried Turkey

Makes 12 servings

1 (10 to 12 lb.) turkey,   2 T. Dijon mustard
   non self-basting   2 T. whiskey
4 to 5 gallons peanut oil   ¼ C. finely chopped
   (see Note 2 on page 1)   pecans, toasted*
¼ C. maple syrup   Salt and pepper to taste
3 T. butter

Remove any plastic bags or pop-up timer from turkey. Remove giblets and neck from turkey and rinse turkey in cold water. Using paper towels, thoroughly dry both outside and inside cavity of turkey. Cut the wing tips from the turkey, as well as small tail, as they may get caught in the fryer basket.

Add measured amount of peanut oil to a 7 to 10 gallon fryer pot (see Note 2 on page 1). Set fryer to medium-high setting and heat oil to 375°F. It should take about 40+ minutes to heat the oil, depending on the amount of oil, outside temperature and wind conditions. Meanwhile, place turkey, neck down, in the turkey fryer basket or on the rack.

When oil temperature reaches 375° on a deep-fry thermometer, slowly lower turkey into the oil (see Note 3 on page 1). Because of frothing caused by the moisture from the turkey, the level of the oil will rise but will stabilize in about 1 minute.

Immediately check the oil temperature and increase the flame so the oil temperature is maintained at 350°. If the oil temperature drops to 340° or below, oil will begin to seep into the turkey.

(Continued on Next Page)

Fry turkey for about 3 to 4 minutes per pound, or about 35 to 42 minutes for a 10 to 12 pound turkey. Be sure to stay near the cooker, as the heat must be closely regulated. Using a meat thermometer, check the temperature of the breast or thigh. When the breast has been cooked to 170°F or the thigh has been cooked to 180°F, carefully remove the turkey from the hot oil and turn off the fryer. Allow the turkey to drain for a few minutes. Remove turkey from rack and place on a serving platter.

While turkey is frying, in a medium saucepan over medium heat, combine maple syrup, butter, Dijon mustard, whiskey and chopped toasted pecans. Bring mixture to a boil, stirring frequently. Reduce heat and let simmer for 2 to 3 minutes. After turkey has drained, spoon glaze over hot turkey. Allow turkey to rest for about 15 minutes before carving. Season with salt and pepper.

Let hot oil cool completely before transferring to storage containers or disposing (see Note 4 on page 1).

*To toast, place finely chopped pecans in a single layer on a baking sheet. Bake at 350° for approximately 10 minutes or until pecans are golden brown.

Onion Stuffed Deep-Fried Turkey with Honey Beer Sauce

Makes 12 servings

1 (10 to 12 lb.) turkey, non self-basting
1 medium yellow onion, cut into ¼" slices
4 to 5 gallons peanut oil (see Note 2 on page 1)

2 T. beer
2 T. honey
2 T. Dijon mustard
1 tsp. fresh chopped thyme

Remove any plastic bags or pop-up timer from turkey. Remove giblets and neck from turkey and rinse turkey in cold water. Using paper towels, thoroughly dry both outside and inside cavity of turkey. Loosen skin over breast area of turkey by carefully slipping fingers between skin and meat. Gently lift the skin and slide onion slices under the skin. Cut the wing tips from the turkey, as well as small tail, as they may get caught in the fryer basket.

Add measured amount of peanut oil to a 7 to 10 gallon fryer pot (see Note 2 on page 1). Set fryer to medium-high setting and heat oil to 375°F. It should take about 40+ minutes to heat the oil, depending on the amount of oil, outside temperature and wind conditions. Meanwhile, place turkey, neck down, in the turkey fryer basket or on the rack.

When oil temperature reaches 375° on a deep-fry thermometer, slowly lower turkey into the oil (see Note 3 on page 1). Because of frothing caused by the moisture from the turkey, the level of the oil will rise but will stabilize in about 1 minute.

(Continued on Next Page)

Immediately check the oil temperature and increase the flame so the oil temperature is maintained at 350°. If the oil temperature drops to 340° or below, oil will begin to seep into the turkey.

Fry turkey for about 3 to 4 minutes per pound, or about 35 to 42 minutes for a 10 to 12 pound turkey. Be sure to stay near the cooker, as the heat must be closely regulated. Using a meat thermometer, check the temperature of the breast or thigh. When the breast has been cooked to 170°F or the thigh has been cooked to 180°F, carefully remove the turkey from the hot oil and turn off the fryer. Allow the turkey to drain for a few minutes. Remove turkey from rack and place on a serving platter.

While turkey is frying, in a small bowl, combine beer, honey, Dijon mustard and fresh chopped thyme. Mix well. After turkey has drained, spoon honey and beer mixture over hot turkey. Allow turkey to rest for about 15 minutes before carving.

Let hot oil cool completely before transferring to storage containers or disposing (see Note 4 on page 1).

How to Carve a Turkey

1. Allow the turkey to rest at least 15 minutes before carving. The turkey can rest up to half an hour, if desired.

2. Get the right carving utensils. A long-pronged fork and a long sharp knife work the best.

3. Place turkey on a large cutting board, breast side up. Hold the turkey with the fork and run the sharp knife down the breastbone on each side of the turkey.

4. Remove the entire breast from the turkey and slice the breast meat crosswise to desired thickness.

5. Using a kitchen towel, hold onto the end of one drumstick with one hand and run the knife between the drumstick and the body of the turkey. Cut through the meat to the joint and twist slightly to remove the drumstick.

6. Remove each wing by cutting between the wing and the frame of the turkey.

7. Present turkey by fanning breast slices out on a serving platter. Place drumsticks and wings on the platter as well. Serve and Enjoy!

Take Your Fryer Camping!

Omelets in a Bag

Makes 30 to 60 servings

Water
1 small Ziplock bag
  per person
2 eggs per person

Shredded Cheddar cheese
Cooked diced bacon
Chopped onions
Chopped green peppers

Fill the turkey fryer pot $\frac{3}{4}$ full with water. Set fryer to medium setting and bring water to a boil. Meanwhile, have each camper put their initials on their Ziplock bag with a permanent marker. Have each camper crack two eggs into their Ziplock bag. Have each camper add shredded cheese, bacon, onions, green peppers, etc., as desired. Seal the bags, working the ingredients together by hand. Release any air from the bags and seal again. When the water is boiling, drop filled bags into water and cook for about 4 minutes, until eggs are fully cooked. Open bags and roll omelets out onto plates.

Corn on the Cob
for a Crowd

Makes 15 to 20 servings

**1 ear of corn for   Water
    each person**

Fill the turkey fryer pot $\frac{3}{4}$ full with water. Set fryer to medium setting and bring water to a boil. Meanwhile, have each camper pull the husks and silk from their ear of corn. Break off the end of each cob. When the water is boiling, carefully drop ears of corn into the water. Boil corn for 6 minutes, until tender. Using a pair of long tongs, remove the corn from the fryer pot and serve.

Fish Fry

Makes about 15 servings

Frying oil	1 C. beer, room
8 to 10 lbs. fish pieces	temperature
1 C. Bisquick baking mix	4 eggs, separated
1 C. cornstarch	2 T. salt

Pour frying oil into fryer pot. Set fryer to medium-high setting and heat oil to 375°F. It should take about 30+ minutes to heat the oil, depending on the amount of oil, outside temperature and wind conditions. Meanwhile, rinse fish pieces and dry thoroughly. In a medium bowl, combine baking mix, cornstarch, beer and egg yolks. Beat egg whites until stiff peaks form and fold egg whites into beer mixture. Coat fish pieces in batter, shaking off excess.

When oil temperature reaches 375° on a deep-fry thermometer, slowly place battered fish pieces into the oil.

Fry fish for about 3 minutes, or until golden. Remove fish from oil with a slotted spoon or using the fryer basket and set on paper towels to drain.

Let hot oil cool completely before transferring to storage containers or disposing (see Note 4 on page 1).

Crispy Potato Skins

Makes 16 servings

16 large baking   Salt and pepper to taste
   potatoes, scrubbed   Sour cream
Frying oil

Before leaving for your camping trip, prick potatoes with a fork and bake in a 400° oven until tender, about 1 hour. Remove potatoes and let cool. Cut baked potatoes in half lengthwise and scoop out potato flesh. Reserve potato flesh for another use. Cut skins in half again.

At campsite, pour frying oil into fryer pot. Set fryer to medium-high setting and heat oil to 375°F. It should take about 30+ minutes to heat the oil, depending on the amount of oil, outside temperature and wind conditions. Meanwhile, sprinkle potato skins with desired amount of salt and pepper.

When oil temperature reaches 375° on a deep-fry thermometer, slowly place potato skins into the oil.

Fry potatoes for about 2 to 3 minutes, or until golden. Remove potatoes from oil with a slotted spoon or using the fryer basket and set on paper towels to drain. Sprinkle with additional salt and pepper to taste. Serve with sour cream for dipping.

Let hot oil cool completely before transferring to storage containers or disposing (see Note 4 on page 1).

Deep Fried Mars Bars

Makes 15 servings

Frying oil
15 Mars or Milky Way
   candy bars
6 C. flour

3 C. corn flour
1 T. baking soda
2 C. milk

Pour frying oil into fryer pot. Set fryer to medium-high setting and heat oil to 350°F. It should take about 20+ minutes to heat the oil, depending on the amount of oil, outside temperature and wind conditions. Meanwhile, in a medium bowl, combine flour, corn flour, baking soda and milk. Mix well and dip candy bars into batter, shaking off excess.

When oil temperature reaches 350° on a deep-fry thermometer, slowly place battered candy bars into the oil.

Fry candy bars for about 30 seconds or until coating is crispy. Remove candy bars from oil with a slotted spoon or using the fryer basket and set on paper towels to drain.

Let hot oil cool completely before transferring to storage containers or disposing (see Note 4 on page 1).

S'mores

Makes 15 servings

30 graham cracker halves	15 pieces of chocolate
	15 marshmallows

Remove turkey fryer pot from turkey fryer. Using only the propane cooking portion of the fryer, set fryer to low heat. Place marshmallows on long sticks and roast over flame to desired doneness. To assemble S'mores, place roasted marshmallow on 1 graham cracker half. Top with 1 piece of chocolate and another graham cracker half to make a sandwich. Enjoy!

The Biggest Cooler

5 to 10 lbs. ice

Canned or bottle beverages

Why not use your turkey fryer as a gigantic cooler? It is the perfect size for a large group and the aluminum fryer pot keeps the ice cold. Fill the turkey fryer pot with 5 to 10 pounds of ice and set canned or bottle beverages tucked into the ice. Cover the pot and set the fryer pot in a shady place. Enjoy cold beverages throughout the day!

Fried Bananas

Makes 24 servings

Frying oil	2 C. whipping cream
2 C. cake flour	12 ripe firm bananas
2 T. sugar	4 C. dry bread crumbs
¼ tsp. salt	Powdered sugar for dusting
2 eggs	

Pour frying oil into fryer pot. Set fryer to medium-high setting and heat oil to 350°F. It should take about 20+ minutes to heat the oil, depending on the amount of oil, outside temperature and wind conditions. Meanwhile, in a large bowl, combine, flour, sugar and salt. In a separate bowl, whisk together eggs and whipping cream. Add egg mixture to flour mixture. Place bread crumbs in a large shallow dish. Peel bananas and cut each banana in half. Dip banana halves in batter and dredge in bread crumbs.

When oil temperature reaches 350° on a deep-fry thermometer, slowly place bananas into the oil.

Fry bananas for about 3 minutes, until golden. Remove bananas from oil with a slotted spoon or using the fryer basket and set on paper towels to drain.

Let hot oil cool completely before transferring to storage containers or disposing (see Note 4 on page 1).

Crispy Catfish

Makes 20 servings

Frying oil
10 lbs. fresh or
    frozen catfish

3 C. buttermilk
1 T. cayenne pepper
3 C. cornmeal

Pour frying oil into fryer pot. Set fryer to medium-high setting and heat oil to 375°F. It should take about 30+ minutes to heat the oil, depending on the amount of oil, outside temperature and wind conditions. Meanwhile, thaw and wash catfish thoroughly. Pat fish dry completely with paper towels. In a medium bowl, place buttermilk. In a large bowl, combine cayenne pepper and cornmeal. Dip catfish in buttermilk and dredge in cornmeal mixture.

When oil temperature reaches 375° on a deep-fry thermometer, slowly place catfish pieces into the oil.

Fry catfish for about 3 to 4 minutes, until golden. Remove catfish from oil with a slotted spoon or using the fryer basket and set on paper towels to drain.

Let hot oil cool completely before transferring to storage containers or disposing (see Note 4 on page 1).

Corn Dogs

Makes 20 corn dogs

Frying oil
2 (16 oz.) pkgs. of
  10 hotdogs
20 (12" or longer)
  wooden dowels
$1\frac{1}{2}$ C. flour

$1\frac{1}{3}$ C. cornmeal
$\frac{1}{4}$ C. sugar
3 tsp. baking powder
$\frac{1}{2}$ tsp. salt
$1\frac{1}{2}$ C. milk
2 eggs

Pour frying oil into fryer pot. Set fryer to medium-high setting and heat oil to 375°F. It should take about 30+ minutes to heat the oil, depending on the amount of oil, outside temperature and wind conditions. Meanwhile, pat hotdogs dry with paper towels. Insert wooden dowels into hotdogs. In a large bowl, combine flour, cornmeal, sugar, baking powder and salt. In a separate bowl, combine milk and eggs. Add milk mixture to cornmeal mixture and stir until well blended. Dip hotdogs into batter mixture until fully coated.

When oil temperature reaches 375° on a deep-fry thermometer, slowly dip corndogs into the oil, holding onto the other end of the corndogs. Be sure to wear heavy rubber gloves to avoid burns from splashing oil.

Fry corndogs for about 2 to 3 minutes, until golden brown. Remove corndogs from oil and set on paper towels to drain and cool.

Let hot oil cool completely before transferring to storage containers or disposing (see Note 4 on page 1).

Camping Donuts

Makes 24 donuts

Frying oil
6 T. shortening
1⅓ C. sugar
4 eggs
7 C. flour
8 tsp. baking powder

2 tsp. salt
½ tsp. cinnamon
¼ tsp. ground cloves
¼ tsp. nutmeg
1⅓ C. milk

Pour frying oil into fryer pot. Set fryer to medium-high setting and heat oil to 400°F. It should take about 40+ minutes to heat the oil, depending on the amount of oil, outside temperature and wind conditions. Meanwhile, in a medium bowl, combine shortening and sugar. Mix in eggs. In a separate bowl, combine flour, baking powder, salt, cinnamon, ground cloves and nutmeg. Alternating, add milk and shortening mixture to dry ingredients, stirring until a stiff dough forms. On a lightly floured flat surface, roll dough to ½" thickness. Using a 3" donut cutter, cut donuts out of dough.

When oil temperature reaches 400° on a deep-fry thermometer, slowly place donuts and donut holes into the oil.

Fry donuts, turning once, until golden on both sides. Remove donuts from oil with a slotted spoon or using the fryer basket and set on paper towels to drain.

Let hot oil cool completely before transferring to storage containers or disposing (see Note 4 on page 1).

Fiesta Chicken Soup

Makes 10 to 12 servings

1 (32 oz.) can chicken broth

2 (14½ oz.) cans whole kernel corn, undrained

1 (14 to 16 oz.) can Ranch style beans

1 (10 oz.) can diced tomatoes with green chilies

2 chicken bouillon cubes

1 (10 oz.) can white chunk chicken, drained

1 (8 oz.) box Velveeta light cheese

Remove the turkey fryer pot from the turkey fryer and place a Dutch oven over the propane cooking portion of the fryer. Set turkey fryer to medium setting. Open all cans and place chicken broth, corn in juice, Ranch style beans, diced tomatoes with green chilies, chicken bouillon cubes and drained white chunk chicken in Dutch oven. Cook mixture, stirring occasionally, until heated throughout, stirring frequently with a long spoon. Cut Velveeta cheese into cubes. Add cheese cubes to soup and stir until cheese is melted.

Corn Bread

Makes 10 to 12 servings

1 C. butter, melted	2 C. cornmeal
4 eggs, beaten	3 C. flour
3 C. milk	4 tsp. baking powder
2 C. sugar	1 tsp. salt

Remove the turkey fryer pot from the turkey fryer and place a Dutch oven over the propane cooking portion of the fryer. Set turkey fryer to low setting. In a large bowl, combine melted butter, eggs and milk. Add sugar, cornmeal, flour, baking powder and salt. Lightly grease the Dutch oven and spoon corn bread mixture into pot. Set Dutch oven over cooking portion of turkey fryer. Place lid on Dutch oven and bake for 45 minutes or until corn bread is golden brown, being careful not to burn.

Camper's Fruit Cobbler

Makes 16 servings

4 (29 oz.) cans sliced
peaches in syrup
4 (30 oz.) cans fruit
cocktail in syrup
4 (20 oz.) cans crushed
pineapple in juice

2 C. instant tapioca
4 (18 oz.) pkgs. white
cake mix
4 C. brown sugar
2 C. butter or margarine

Remove the turkey fryer pot from the turkey fryer and place a Dutch oven over the propane cooking portion of the fryer. Set turkey fryer to low setting. Line the Dutch oven with aluminum foil. Open all cans and add sliced peaches in syrup, fruit cocktail in syrup, crushed pineapple in juice and instant tapioca to Dutch oven. Set Dutch oven over cooking portion of turkey fryer. Sprinkle white cake mixes over fruit and tapioca and sprinkle brown sugar over cake mix. Dab pieces of butter over brown sugar. Place lid on Dutch oven and bake cobbler for 45 to 60 minutes, being careful not to burn. The cobbler is done when cake mix has absorbed the juices and is no longer dry.

Dish Washer

Water   **Dish soap**

Your turkey fryer can double as a large dish washer pot when you are away from home. Just fill the turkey fryer pot half full with water. Set the fryer to low heat and warm the water. When the water reaches desired temperature (being careful not to boil), add dish soap. Wash all your dirty camping dishes in one large pot. Be sure to rinse the turkey fryer after washing dishes to remove any soap residue from the pot.

Works Great for Wok Recipes!

Cooking with a Wok

You can use your turkey fryer to make wok recipes by removing the turkey fryer pot and place the wok directly over the propane cooking portion of the turkey fryer. The heat will cook the foods within the wok quickly and evenly, making a great meal in just a few minutes!

Choose a wok that is heavy and deep. Woks made of carbon steel are preferred, as stainless steel, Teflon-coated woks and electric woks are discouraged because it is difficult to control the source of heat and foods often stick to the surface.

Make sure the wok is fully heated before adding the ingredients. Pour oil into the wok and swirl to coat the sides. Normally, foods such as poultry, seafood or tofu should be cooked before adding vegetables.

Use a spatula or wooden spoon to stir the foods in the wok, making sure to stir the ingredients every couple seconds. Keeping the food moving will prevent the foods from sticking to the bottom of the wok. To take advantage of the entire cooking surface, make sure to spread the foods around the entire wok instead of keeping the foods in the center.

Clean your heated wok with only water and a soft sponge. Do not wipe your wok entirely clean.

Garlic Beef

1 T. vegetable oil
8 cloves garlic, minced
$\frac{1}{4}$ C. soy sauce
2 T. sesame oil
2 T. apple cider vinegar
2 T. sugar
$\frac{1}{2}$ tsp. pepper

1 lb. flank steak, thinly sliced
1 lb. fresh green beans, trimmed
1 red bell pepper, cut into thin strips

Prepare wok by placing wok directly over propane cooking portion of the turkey fryer. Add vegetable oil to wok, swirling to coat the surface.

In a medium bowl, combine minced garlic, soy sauce, sesame oil, vinegar, sugar and pepper.

Add sliced steak to heated wok and cook for 5 to 6 minutes, stirring frequently, until cooked throughout. Add green beans, red pepper strips and soy sauce mixture. Stir-fry for about 10 minutes, until green beans are tender but crisp and most of the liquid has been absorbed. Serve immediately.

107

Orange-Ginger Beef Stir-Fry

Makes 4 servings

1 T. vegetable oil
¾ lb. flank steak,
   thinly sliced
2 tsp. cornstarch
3 T. orange marmalade
¾ tsp. ground ginger
1 (10 oz.) pkg. frozen
   broccoli florets,
   thawed

1 (8 oz.) can water
   chestnuts, drained
¼ C. soy sauce
2 C. cooked brown rice
¼ C. dry roasted
   peanuts

Prepare wok by placing wok directly over propane cooking portion of the turkey fryer. Add vegetable oil to wok, swirling to coat the surface.

In a medium bowl, place steak strips. Add cornstarch and toss until coated. Add orange marmalade and ginger and stir until evenly coated.

Add steak mixture to heated wok and cook for 4 to 5 minutes, stirring frequently, until cooked throughout. Add broccoli, drained water chestnuts and soy sauce. Cover wok and let mixture simmer for about 5 minutes, until thickened, stirring frequently. Serve over rice and sprinkle with peanuts.

Steak Stir-Fry

Makes 4 servings

2 T. vegetable oil, divided 1 clove garlic, minced
1 tsp. beef bouillon   1 tsp. ground ginger
1 C. boiling water $\frac{1}{4}$ tsp. pepper
2 T. cornstarch   1 green pepper, thinly
$\frac{1}{3}$ C. soy sauce   sliced
1 lb. boneless sirloin   1 C. sliced celery
    steak, cut into thin   5 green onions, chopped
    strips

Prepare wok by placing wok directly over propane cooking portion of the turkey fryer. Add 1 tablespoon vegetable oil to wok, swirling to coat the surface.

In a medium bowl, combine beef bouillon and boiling water, stirring until bouillon is completely dissolved. In a small bowl, combine cornstarch and soy sauce and add to bouillon mixture. In a separate bowl, toss together steak strips, minced garlic, ground ginger and pepper.

Add steak mixture to heated wok and cook for 4 to 5 minutes, stirring frequently, until cooked throughout. Remove cooked steak from wok and keep warm. Add remaining 1 tablespoon vegetable oil to wok and stir in green pepper slices, sliced celery and chopped green onions. Stir-fry until vegetables are tender and stir in soy sauce mixture. Bring mixture to a boil and cook for 2 minutes, stirring frequently. Return cooked steak to wok and stir-fry until heated throughout. Serve immediately.

Honey Chicken Stir-Fry

Makes 6 servings

2 tsp. peanut oil
1 T. cornstarch
¾ C. orange juice
3 T. soy sauce
1 T. honey
1 tsp. fresh minced
  gingerroot

2 stalks celery, chopped
2 carrots, peeled and
  sliced
1½ lbs. boneless,
  skinless chicken breast
  halves, cut into strips
¼ C. minced green onions

Prepare wok by placing wok directly over propane cooking portion of the turkey fryer. Add peanut oil to wok, swirling to coat the surface.

In a small bowl, combine cornstarch and orange juice, mixing until cornstarch is completely dissolved. Mix in soy sauce, honey and gingerroot.

Add chopped celery and sliced carrots to heated wok and cook for about 3 minutes, stirring frequently, until tender. Add chicken pieces and stir-fry for an additional 5 minutes. Add orange juice mixture and minced green onions and cook, stirring frequently, until thickened.

Paella

1 T. vegetable oil
10 (4 oz.) hot Italian
   sausage links, cut
   into pieces
4 boneless, skinless
   chicken breast halves,
   cut into strips
1 onion, chopped
1 green bell pepper,
   cut into strips
1 stalk celery, finely
   chopped

2 cloves garlic, minced
2 (14½ oz.) cans
   peeled diced tomatoes,
   drained
2 bay leaves
2 tsp. salt
1 tsp. dried oregano
¾ tsp. ground turmeric
3½ C. chicken broth
2 lbs. large shrimp,
   peeled and deveined

Prepare wok by placing wok directly over propane cooking portion of the turkey fryer. Add vegetable oil to wok, swirling to coat the surface.

Add sausage pieces to heated wok and cook, stirring frequently, until browned on all sides. Remove sausage pieces and add chicken pieces and stir-fry for about 5 minutes. Remove chicken pieces and add chopped onions, green bell pepper strips, chopped celery, minced garlic, drained tomatoes, bay leaves, salt, oregano, turmeric and chicken broth. Stir-fry until heated throughout and vegetables are tender, about 15 minutes.

Add sausage pieces, chicken and shrimp to wok and cook until heated throughout and shrimp is cooked throughout. Serve immediately.

Beef & Broccoli

Makes 6 servings

1 T. vegetable oil
¾ C. beef broth
1 T. soy sauce
1 tsp. garlic powder
¼ tsp. ground ginger
½ tsp. pepper
1 T. brown sugar

1 T. cornstarch
1 lb. bottom round steak,
   cut into strips
2 medium onions, cut
   into wedges
1 bunch broccoli, cut
   into florets

Prepare wok by placing wok directly over propane cooking portion of the turkey fryer. Add vegetable oil to wok, swirling to coat the surface.

In a medium bowl, combine beef broth, soy sauce, garlic powder, ginger, pepper, brown sugar and cornstarch. Mix well and set aside.

Add steak to heated wok and cook for 4 to 5 minutes, stirring frequently, until cooked throughout. Add onions and broccoli and stir-fry for an additional 3 to 4 minutes, until onions are tender. Add beef broth mixture and cook, stirring constantly, for 2 to 3 minutes, until the sauce is thickened. Serve immediately.

Garlic Chicken Stir-Fry

Makes 4 servings

2 T. peanut oil
1 C. chicken broth, divided
2 T. soy sauce
2 T. sugar
2 T. cornstarch
6 cloves garlic, minced, divided
1 tsp. fresh grated gingerroot
4 green onions, chopped
1 tsp. salt
1 lb. boneless, skinless chicken breasts, cut into strips
2 onions, thinly sliced
1 C. shredded cabbage
1 red bell pepper, thinly sliced
2 C. sugar snap peas

Prepare wok by placing wok directly over propane cooking portion of the turkey fryer. Add peanut oil to wok, swirling to coat the surface.

In a small bowl, combine $\frac{1}{2}$ cup chicken broth, soy sauce, sugar and cornstarch.

Add 2 minced garlic cloves, grated gingerroot, chopped green onions and salt to heated wok and cook for about 2 minutes, stirring frequently, until cooked throughout. Add chicken and stir-fry for an additional 3 to 4 minutes, until chicken is cooked throughout. Add remaining 4 minced garlic cloves, sliced onions, shredded cabbage, sliced red bell peppers, sugar snap peas and remaining $\frac{1}{2}$ cup chicken broth and cover wok. Add sauce mixture to skillet and stir-fry until vegetables are heated and well coated. Serve immediately.

Kung Pao Beef

Makes 6 to 8 servings

1 T. vegetable oil
½ C. teriyaki sauce
1 tsp. crushed red
   pepper
2 T. cornstarch

½ tsp. ground ginger
2 lbs. flank steak,
   thinly sliced
⅔ C. salted peanuts
4 green onions, chopped

Prepare wok by placing wok directly over propane cooking portion of the turkey fryer. Add vegetable oil to wok, swirling to coat the surface.

In a large bowl, combine teriyaki sauce, crushed red pepper, cornstarch and ground ginger. Add sliced steak and toss until coated.

Add steak mixture to heated wok and cook for 5 to 7 minutes, stirring frequently, until cooked throughout. Add salted peanuts and chopped green onions and stir until heated throughout.

114

Sesame Shrimp Stir-Fry

Makes 4 servings

2 T. sesame oil
1 lb. mediums shrimp, peeled and deveined
¼ tsp. ground ginger
¼ tsp. cayenne pepper
1 clove garlic, minced
1 T. sesame seeds
¼ tsp. pepper

1 red bell pepper, thinly sliced
3 green onions, chopped
3 T. teriyaki sauce
½ lb. sugar snap peas
⅛ C. cornstarch
¾ C. chicken broth
¼ tsp. salt

Prepare wok by placing wok directly over propane cooking portion of the turkey fryer. Add sesame oil to wok, swirling to coat the surface.

In a large bowl, combine shrimp, ground ginger, cayenne pepper, minced garlic, sesame seeds and pepper.

Add red bell pepper slices and chopped green onions to heated wok and cook for 3 to 4 minutes, stirring frequently, until softened. Add teriyaki sauce, sugar snap peas and shrimp mixture and stir until heated throughout and shrimp turn opaque. In a small bowl, combine cornstarch and chicken broth. Add chicken broth mixture to wok and sprinkle with salt. Serve immediately.

Mediterranean Vegetables

Makes 4 servings

2 T. olive oil
5 cloves garlic, minced
1 onion, thinly sliced
4 green, red or yellow
   bell peppers, thinly
   sliced

2 medium zucchini, sliced
3 T. capers in juice
2 tsp. fresh chopped
   basil
Salt and pepper to taste

Prepare wok by placing wok directly over propane cooking portion of the turkey fryer. Add olive oil to wok, swirling to coat the surface.

Add minced garlic, sliced onions, sliced peppers and sliced zucchinis to heated wok and cook for 2 to 3 minutes, stirring frequently, until vegetables are tender but crisp. Stir in capers in juice, chopped basil, salt and pepper. Cook until heated and serve immediately.

Sautéed Green Beans

Makes 4 servings

2 slices thick bacon,
   cut into 1" pieces
1 small onion, diced
1 lb. green beans,
   trimmed
1 clove garlic, minced

$\frac{1}{3}$ C. water
$\frac{1}{2}$ tsp. dried thyme
$\frac{1}{2}$ tsp. salt
1 T. balsamic vinegar
Pepper

Prepare wok by placing wok directly over propane cooking portion of the turkey fryer. When wok is heated, add bacon pieces to wok and cooked until evenly browned and crisp. Remove bacon from wok and keep warm.

Add diced onions to heated wok and stir-fry for about 5 minutes. Add green beans, minced garlic, water, dried thyme and salt. Increase heat and stir-fry for about 5 minutes, cooking until beans are bright in color and just tender. Stir in cooked bacon, balsamic vinegar and pepper.

Mongolian Turkey

Makes 4 to 6 servings

1 T. vegetable oil
3 C. stemmed broccoli
    florets
2 green onions, chopped
1 red bell pepper,
    thinly sliced
2 T. fresh grated
    gingerroot
2 cloves garlic, minced
3 C. cooked turkey,
    cut into $\frac{1}{2}$" strips

$1\frac{1}{2}$ C. turkey or
    chicken broth, divided
$\frac{1}{3}$ C. soy sauce
$\frac{1}{4}$ C. dry sherry
2 T. sesame oil
$\frac{3}{4}$ tsp. peppercorns
$\frac{1}{3}$ tsp. crushed red
    pepper flakes
1 T. plus 1 tsp.
    cornstarch

Prepare wok by placing wok directly over propane cooking portion of the turkey fryer. Add vegetable oil to wok, swirling to coat the surface.

Add stemmed broccoli, chopped green onions, sliced peppers, gingerroot and minced garlic. Stir until onions and broccoli are tender and add cooked turkey strips and $\frac{1}{2}$ cup turkey or chicken broth and continue to stir-fry for 2 minutes.

In a medium bowl, combine remaining 1 cup turkey broth, soy sauce, dry sherry, sesame oil, peppercorns and red pepper flakes. Add cornstarch and mix with a whisk until well combined. Add cornstarch mixture to wok and cook until sauce is thickened.

Garlic Mushrooms

Makes 4 servings

¾ lb. button
   mushrooms
4 baby bok choy,
   halved lengthwise
2 T. dry sherry

1 T. oyster sauce
2 tsp. soy sauce
2 T. vegetable oil
1 T. minced garlic
1 tsp. sesame oil

In a large pot of boiling water, cook mushrooms for 2 minutes. Remove mushrooms with a slotted spoon and rinse under cold water. Add bok choy to boiling water and cook for 30 seconds to 1 minute, until tender but crisp. Drain and rinse under cold water.

In a small bowl, combine dry sherry, oyster sauce and soy sauce.

Prepare wok by placing wok directly over propane cooking portion of the turkey fryer. Add vegetable oil to wok, swirling to coat the surface.

Add mushrooms, bok choy and minced garlic to heat wok and stir-fry for about 2 minutes. Stir in sesame oil and dry sherry mixture and stir-fry for an additional minute.

Cashew Chicken

Makes 6 servings

¼ C. vegetable oil
⅓ C. cornstarch
½ C. cold water
2 C. diced chicken meat
1 tsp. salt
½ tsp. pepper
3 C. chicken broth
2 T. soy sauce

1 C. chopped celery
1 (8 oz.) can bamboo
  shoots, drained
  and diced
1 (8 oz.) can water
  chestnuts, drained
1 C. cashews

Prepare wok by placing wok directly over propane cooking portion of the turkey fryer. Add vegetable oil to wok, swirling to coat the surface.

In a small bowl, combine cornstarch and cold water, stirring until cornstarch is dissolved.

Add chicken, salt, pepper, chicken broth, soy sauce, chopped celery, diced bamboo shoots and drained water chestnuts to heated wok and cook for about 5 minutes, stirring frequently. Stir in cornstarch mixture, until thickened and divide mixture onto plates. Sprinkle some of the cashews over each serving.

INDEX

IDEAS & RECIPES FOR SPRING

IDEAS & RECIPES FOR SUMMER

IDEAS & RECIPES FOR FALL

IDEAS & RECIPES FOR WINTER

YUMMY TURKEY RECIPES

TAKE YOUR FRYER CAMPING

WORKS GREAT FOR WOK RECIPES!